HOLES IN A
STAINED

GLASS

WINDOW

NORMAN CORWIN

LYLE STUART INC.

Secaucus, N.J.

Some of these texts expand on articles that
appeared originally in *Westways Magazine*, the
Los Angeles Times, and *PHP*. *Prayer for the 70s*
was published as a mini-book by Doubleday, and
The Few Appropriate Remarks appeared in the
anthology *Lincoln for the Ages*. Grateful
acknowledgment is hereby made.

N. C.

Queries regarding rights and permissions should
be addressed to Lyle Stuart Inc., 120 Enterprise
Ave., Secaucus, N. J. 07094.

Published by Lyle Stuart Inc. Published simultaneously
in Canada by George J. McLeod Limited, Toronto, Ont.
Manufactured in the United States of America

Design by Janet Anderson

Library of Congress Cataloging in Publication Data
Corwin, Norman Lewis, 1910-
   Holes in a stained glass window.
   I. Title.
PS3505.0777H6   811'.5'2   77-13791
ISBN O-8184-0255-5

§ § § § § § § § § §

Dedicated with esteem and affection to
RAY BRADBURY,
friend of many years. For further
details see *Mailbox on Mars* herein.

CONTENTS

§ § § § MEDIA, EQUIVOKES, SNOBS, PIFFLE

§ § § § § § § § § § § JERUSALEM PRINTOUT

§ § § § §

*The trouble with stained glass windows is
you can't see through them.*

You'd have to punch holes in it.

— cab driver, Philadelphia

§ § § § §

ON
WRITERS AND
§ § § § § § WRITING § § § § §

OF CHAUCER, MILTON AND SKYWRITERS

POETS OF THE WORLD SHOULD UNITE IN GRATI-
tude to Rod McKuen for disclosing not only that poetry can
be profitable but that a poet's name leads the list of all writers
of all media of all times in hard-cover sales.

The authority for this stunning statistic is McKuen himself.
Invited by the *Los Angeles Times* to discuss in print what poets
are and are not, he sent in his article along with a biographical
note which read as follows:

> *Having sold more than ten million books of poetry in
> hard cover in the past ten years, Rod McKuen is consid-
> ered not only the best selling poet of all time, but the
> best selling author writing in any medium in hard cover.
> In addition, he is a classical composer nominated for the
> Pulitzer Prize in music in 1974.*

As a sometime poet myself who has sold 9,987,869 fewer

copies of hard-cover verse than Mr. McKuen over the past 20 years, I rejoice in his success. The scope and sweep of his achievement can best be appreciated if you savor the awesome span of centuries expressed in the phrase "of all time." This would include the Assyrian poets who wrote on stone tablets (certainly hard covers if there ever were any), and the Imhotep School of ancient Egyptian poets centered in Abydos (2nd Dynasty), who were published in volumes of papyrus pressed between slabs of wood. The total sales of the entire Imhotep School, numbering 117 poets, and even counting a score of their apprentices whose work was released in soft cover (crocodile skin) through a quarterly entitled *Aswat Aneel Al Jadida* (New Voices of the Nile) amounted to only 186 copies, mostly bought by relatives and friends of the authors.

Some idea of the weight of McKuen's sales may be seen in the relatively mournful numbers respecting Chaucer (b. 1343) and Milton (d. 1675). The former, often called "the father of English poetry," sold only 374 copies of his *Canterbury Tales* in his lifetime, even though his publisher pushed hard on the bawdy content, trying to appeal to the lusty appetites of the period. Milton, on the other hand, was helped by the book clubs which sprang up around London in 1667, and still he could get rid of only 753 copies of *Paradise Lost*. This figure included complimentary copies to reviewers and various girlfriends.

What makes the McKuen record even more remarkable is that it establishes him as the best-selling author writing in *any* medium in hard cover. Printed books are one thing, but today's range of publications encompasses media that were never dreamed of by Milton nor conceived by Gutenberg when he invented movable type.

Take skywriting, which, it goes without saying, is a highly

public form of publication. In more ways than one, skywriting is written on the wind, and counts for almost nothing in hardcover sales.

Then there are the authors who write for fortune cookies and greeting cards. While these two media begin to be competitive in terms of large numbers, they too must be ruled out as being beyond the purview of McKuen's legitimate claims, since neither cookies nor cards can pretend to be hard covered.

There may be scorners who object that the Bible has outsold McKuen, but it is not fair to make this comparison because the Bible is the work of many authors, and it gets free advertising, week in and week out, year after year, from every pulpit in Christendom. So McKuen is 100% correct when he declares that he is the best-selling author of all time of all media in hard cover.

Actually there may be more than a touch of modesty in this self-description, since the *soft*-cover returns on the sale of his books is not all in yet and it is well known that when hardcover titles sell in the millions, the soft-cover followup could reach the billions. I suspect that McKuen's innate good taste enjoined him from making the soft-cover claim at this time. Instead, he quietly called attention to his nomination for a Pulitzer Prize in classical music.

I am glad he mentioned that, because I hate to be ignorant of the emergence of classical composers. There are so few in our midst that they must be welcomed and cherished. Everybody knows how hard it is for new symphonies, cantatas, string quartets and sonatas to be published in hard cover, or for that matter in any cover. (Luckily for me, I may have heard the McKuen First in E-flat minor—known, I believe, as *The Glendale*—if indeed that is the title of a symphony I caught on radio the other night. Static garbled the name of the composer, but it sounded to me like either Rod McKuen or Rock Manin-off—something like that. It was glorious.)

My admiration for McKuen is so boundless that I must restrain myself from dilating on the text of his definition of poets, which was the occasion of his biographical sketch. But perhaps I may indulge myself to the extent of quoting two of his lines of abjuration as to the proper function of a poet:

> *He must repair but never rape the words that form his native tongue . . . nor should he be an advertisement for himself.*

How true that is, Rod McKuen! My words have often needed repair, and I shamefully confess to having committed rape on phrases here and there—although in each instance the phrase was above the age of consent.

But writing *advertisements* for myself I could never bring myself to do, notwithstanding my qualifications of experience in all the media including hard cover, my talents as a painter of murals and composer of madrigals (neither of which, however, has been nominated for anything), my passable charisma, my willingness to travel and my availability for commissions to write want ads, wedding announcements, and letters to editors. My rates are not exorbitant, and I can be reached at any time of day or night through the Writers Guild of America, West, Inc., 8955 Beverly Boulevard, Los Angeles, 90048.

DEAR SIR OR MADAM

NAPOLEON ONCE INSTRUCTED HIS SECRETARY to leave all letters unopened for three weeks, by which time a large part of the correspondence would have disposed of itself and no longer would require an answer. The same cynicism about incoming mail was shared by a man not otherwise mentionable in the same breath—Henry Thoreau, who grumbled that he had received no more than one or two letters in his life that were worth the postage.

One need not feel sorry for Napoleon about anything, but it's too bad about Thoreau. Considering the people he knew, you'd think he would have gotten some exciting letters. But since Ralph Waldo Emerson lived in the same town, perhaps they met so often they had no need to write each other. In any case Emerson had a higher regard for the form than his neighbor:

The tongue is prone to lose the way,
Not so the pen, for in a letter
We have not better things to say,
But surely say them better.

Attitudes toward receiving and answering mail vary widely, from the lonely soul who is so hungry for communication that even postal junk is welcome, to the mail snob who considers himself above all correspondence save with his bank and the tax tanks.

As could be expected, writers have more respect for letter-writing than any other class, because they know how much craft is required. Blaise Pascal, 17th Century philosopher, apologized that he had made a letter longer than usual because he lacked the time to make it short. (But then Pascal had a thing about shortness. In his *Pensées,* he wrote that if Cleopatra's nose had been shorter, the whole history of the world would have been different. Not better, just different.) My favorite short-reply model is that of Patrick Dennis, author of *Auntie Mame,* whose standard response to critical correspondents went:

Dear Sir: Thank you for your crank letter.

Gloria Emerson, author of a harrowing book on the Vietnam war, *Winners and Losers,* takes her mail very seriously. She carries a box of it on her travels to promote the book, and answers letters personally on rented typewriters between media interviews. A reporter in Los Angeles wrote that she had 270 letters with her at the time of their interview, and that she intended to answer them all. "If people write to you," she said, "you are morally obliged to answer. If you write a book that's a calling-out, to ignore the answer is to repudiate your own effort."

Another writer who kept careful count was novelist Kenneth Roberts. He was almost obsessed by letter-writing. The measure of his zealotry lay not in the number of letters he wrote, most of which were related to his work, but in the way he kept ultra-fastidious tally of them. In his book of memoirs, *I Wanted to Write,* he takes up ten whole pages with a *list* of people and parties to whom he dispatched letters during a whole year. On December 19, for example, he logs:

> *de Bois*
> *Laurent*
> *& 12 postcards*

and, scattered throughout the roster, are letters to Mother, 2nd National, Brooks Bros., Cal. potato man, and Aspergum Co. Even when Roberts was in such an enchanting spot as Porto Santo Stefano, in Italy, where one would hope he might relax a little, he doggedly kept score. A diary entry reports that he dictated 81 letters in one month, and that his secretary turned out 50 of her own. Perhaps not since Thomas Jefferson, who wrote over 50,000 letters and kept copies of most of them, has there been such assiduousness in this respect.

At the opposite extreme, some people are indifferent to a point of rudeness about acknowledging mail, even when the correspondent may have high standing. I once got a letter from James Cagney, in which he relayed a request from Judge Benjamin Lindsey, jurist and world renowned authority on juvenile delinquency:

> *Judge Ben Lindsey wrote me asking for a copy of the script. I left mine at the studio. If you will please send one on here I will see that the old guy gets it. If he does, it will be the first time he has ever had an answer from*

anybody in the movies or the radio. He's sore as hell, so
let's cool him off.

Lateness in answering mail is as understandable as it is common. Pressure of work, absence, illness, procrastination are often responsible. But persistently ignoring legitimate correspondence is on the boorish side, and sometimes deserves rebuke, as in the case of A., who had helped a young and aspiring director, B. After A. had repeatedly, and in pain, written B. requesting the return of some material he had lent him, A. wrote:

> *I congratulate you on being able to afford the luxury of*
> *alienating people friendly to your career. That indicates*
> *the security of arrival, which is the goal of every artist.*

The material came back by the next post.

It has been said that a letter shows the person it is written to as well as the person it is written by. But there are so many kinds of letters, so many species and sub-species, that one cannot lightly generalize. For example, to write a good love letter, according to Jean Jacques Rousseau, you should begin without knowing what you want to say, and end without knowing what you have written. A contemporary of Rousseau, the moralist Joubert, felt that "the true character of epistolary style is playfulness and urbanity." I have certainly found that to be true of a good deal of correspondence between people in the performing media, and in letters between artists dating long before movies and TV. The great John Keats, whose mien was mostly sober, and whose writing was sometimes drugged with opulence, as in such lines as

> *What misery most drowningly doth sing*
> *In lone Endymion's ear, now he has raught*
> *The goal of consciousness?*

could unbend delightfully when writing letters. During a trip
to Scotland he wrote his sister a letter containing a poem of
118 short lines, the last stanza of which went

> *There was a naughty Boy*
>   *And a naughty Boy was he,*
> *He ran away to Scotland*
>   *The people for to see—*
>   *Then he found*
>   *That the ground*
>   *Was as hard,*
>   *That a yard*
>   *Was as long,*
>   *That a song*
>   *Was as merry,*
>   *That a cherry*
>   *Was as red—*
>   *That lead*
>   *Was as weighty*
>   *That fourscore*
>   *Was as eighty,*
>   *That a door*
>   *Was as wooden*
>   *As in England—*
>   *So he stood in his shoes*
>   *And he wonder'd,*
>   *He wonder'd,*
>   *He stood in his shoes*
>   *And he wonder'd.*

Byron, too. The same playfulness was in his letters. Most of us,
writing a friend, might ask, "How are you, and what are you
doing?" in just those words. But Byron, addressing the poet
Thomas Moore from Venice, put it this way:

What are you doing now,
  Oh Thomas Moore?
What are you doing now,
  Oh Thomas Moore?

Sighing or suing now?
Rhyming or wooing now?
Billing or cooing now?
  Which, Thomas Moore?

Of course playfulness in letters does not have to take poetic form. Prose can do quite well. The late Deems Taylor, composer and critic whom younger readers may best remember as master of the animated revels in *Fantasia*, once asked my opinion of some verse, and after I had responded, he wrote

> *Mark Twain, upon being shown a photograph of Lillian Russell, is said to have observed, "I would rather be in bed with that woman, with nothing on, than with General Grant in his full dress uniform."*
>   *I feel a little that way about your letter. I'd rather have word from you, who know something about verse, than from Dame Edith Sitwell, who doesn't sit well with me.*

I am sure Mr. Taylor believed, as I do, that Dame Edith knew a lot more about verse than I, but he was not going to pass up an opportunity to pun on her name.

While letters have always been a rich and rewarding literary form, they seldom are of service to drama. Several attempts were made to adapt letters for the stage, notably the exchanges between Jefferson and Adams, and Shaw and Terry, but the essences were too cerebral and static to make good theater. A moving letter from the doomed Bartolomeo Vanzetti was used to powerful effect in *The Male Animal*, but it was by no means central to the play. The letters of Vincent van Gogh to his brother Theo formed the spine of the movie *Lust For Life,* but the restraint with which they were used, and their confinement to the function of cohesive agent, made them work, whereas had they been intrusive they would have weakened rather than supported the structure of the film.

Some fascinating volumes of letters are in the world's libraries, mostly those written by Men of Letters (Cicero, Pliny, Dostoevsky, Dickens, Carlyle, Walpole, Galsworthy, Browning, Frost, Sandburg, Faulkner, Cowley, etc.), but also by persons other than writers. Random House published a handsomely illustrated two-volume edition of *The Letters of the Great Artists,* meaning painters and sculptors, and what most of these letters lack in literary finesse they more than make up through insight to art. Composers, too, have now and then been highly articulate, and their letters worth perpetuating (Berlioz, Schumann, Wagner, Liszt, Stravinsky); but there have also been people little identified with media (if that term may be projected backwards into history)—worthies like St. Paul, Abelard and Heloise, Madame de Sévigne, Jan Hus, and, of course, Chesterfield.

But for every published letter, there are a thousand unpublished that would make good reading, and the number constantly grows. A friend of mine, highly educated, is scandalized at the idea of ever *saving* a letter, even a well-written one, and immediately destroys each after reading it. Not a few people share that view, but the wise old bird who wrote *Faust* begs to differ:

> *We lay aside letters never to read them again, and at last we destroy them out of discretion, and so disappears the most beautiful, the most immediate breath of life, irrecoverably for ourselves and for others.*

Thank you, Dr. Goethe. We will hold onto our files.

WANTED:

PHRASEMAKERS

SOMETHING HAS HAPPENED TO THE PHRASE. It has disappeared from politics and the arts, and seems to hide out, with meager existence, in the shantytowns of slang and patois.

Now and then, when I dip into those massive reservoirs of thunderous phrases on everyone's shelf—the Bible and Shakespeare—I wonder what on earth accounts for the infrequency of impassioned language, of puissant sentences, vivid images, the epigram, the riposte, the long throw of hyperole, the polemic that explodes like Krakatoa.

Are they old-fashioned? Do they belong among the wrecks and monuments of antiquity? Have they no place on the market? Are they effete? Why does contemporary poetry, the last reserve of the phrase, sell so badly that Robert Frost, in all his years, never approached a thousandth part of the circulation of Mickey Spillane?

24

Wanted: Phrasemakers

There was a day, not so long ago, when a novelist left no page unmarked by a phrase that would snap your head as it went by. *Moby Dick* is hardly three sentences along, before Ishmael is saying:

> *Whenever it is a damp, drizzly November in my soul*

And in his first description, less than a paragraph later, Melville writes:

> *There now is your insular city of the Manhattoes, belted round by wharves as Indian isles by coral reefs—commerce surrounds it with her surf.*

Lord knows ours is not a dull generation nor an inarticulate one: we have fine playwrights, novelists and poets, a public that supports the theater at prices up to $17.50 a seat, and book buyers to make rich men of authors who write about sea gulls and sex. But in all the boil and bubble of our culture and economics, the phrase has no real home.

The truth is that heightened language has become suspect. Most editors, producers, and entrepreneurs keep vigil against it. Unless a phrase of any power is couched in colloquial and conventional terms, unless it scrupulously avoids any glimmer of eloquence, it is banished as "purple." Actors are culpable, too. Not the eager, job-hungry new actors, but the complacent "arrived" ones. Some of them tend to be lazy, insisting that lines and phrases be reduced to their own capacities. Often they complain to directors that a speech "does not feel right," that they are not "comfortable" with a certain word or phrase, as though it were the highest function of the playwright to cushion actors with the familiar and expected.

As often as not, when the phrase of a skilled writer does not feel right to an actor, it is an admission of the actor's ignorance, his fear of challenge, or his low artistic ceiling. In the theater he is generally told to put up or shut up, for the author has formidable rights and powers there. But in films, the star system still being in force, it is the line and not the actor's mind that gets changed.

The public, if given a chance, will go far to hear the kind of thunder that lately has been muffled. *Don Juan in Hell* indicated how hungry people are for rich language and ideas, even when framed in the barest production. The Phrase has all but dropped out of the performing arts, and has retreated to the fringes of journalism and politics. In serious literature it is kept alive mostly by a dwindling cadre of poets who have to support themselves as teachers, librarians and doctors, and who are lucky to sell 500 copies of a book of good verse in this land of 200 millions.

Politically, the pickings have been scant since Churchill. Franklin D. Roosevelt's "The only thing we have to fear is fear itself"; Eisenhower's "military-industrial complex"; JFK's "Ask not what your country can do for you—ask what you can do for your country" are about it. How many more than these can be readily recalled? On the other hand, Churchill sparked phrases the way Sancho Panza tossed off proverbs:

> *I have nothing to offer but blood, toil, tears and sweat.*

> *Never in the field of human conflict was so much owed by so many to so few.*

A settled habitat of the Phrase is Madison Avenue, where it lives in a penthouse and works for advertising agencies. Here it is put to work mesmerizing multitudes until it can be burbled by children in their sleep:

Wanted: Phrasemakers

You can be sure if it's Westinghouse.

Get your hands on a Toyota and you'll never let go.

It's not nice to fool with Mother Nature.

Try it, you'll like it.

When you get back to basics, you get back to Ford.

Drive a Datsun, then decide.

Bayer works wonders.

Nothing purple *there*.

Of course truly excessive purple writing is properly scorned. Shakespeare, the greatest phrasemaker of all time, gave a bad notice to:

> *Taffeta phrases, silken terms precise,*
> *Three-pil'd hyperboles, spruce affectation,*
> *Figures pedantical. . . .*

But it takes substance to create dimension. Noble sentiment, powerful language or exalted statement can come only from authors of stature. Nobody would think of calling Jesus Christ's language purple, yet his phrases are among the loftiest ever uttered:

> *O ye hypocrites, ye can discern the face of the sky, but can ye not discern the signs of the times?*

> *What therefore God hath joined together let no man put asunder.*

Purple means heavy or flossy or turgid or obscure. Was the

author of the Book of Job purple? Would an editor or producer of a religious program on TV accept from a staff writer
the following astronomical passage:

> Canst thou bind the sweet influences of the Pleiades, or
> loose the bands of Orion? . . .
> Canst thou guide Arcturus with his sons?

Would the producer permit a description of a horse to get
mixed up in a theosophical discussion—or if he did, would
he allow his writer to soar over the head of his Trendex-rated
audience with this kind of writing:

> Hast thou given the horse strength?
> Hast thou clothed his neck with thunder?
> Canst thou make him afraid as a grasshopper?
> The glory of his nostrils is terrible . . .
> He swalloweth the ground with fierceness and rage . . .
> He saith among the trumpets, Ha ha. . . .

What? The glory of his *nostrils*? What's glorious about nostrils, unless they're Elizabeth Taylor's?

Naturally the kind of phrase that makes the loudest thunder
is the hortatory, and in our generation this has suffered a miser-
able decline. World War I produced a few fair ones:

> Hoch the Kaiser!
> Remember the Lusitania!
> We Won't Be Back Till It's Over Over There!

but World War II's best offering was:

> Praise the Lord and pass the ammunition!

The Vietnam War has contributed only pale and awkward
military circumlocutions, like "protective reaction" and (to
describe a shovel) "combat emplacement evacuator." Of eu-

phemisms there is no end; but mainly we plod along today with pale phrases. Our plays and movies, freed from traditional restraints, enjoy access to the racy domains of the four-letter-word, and some writers seem not to be able to function without it. Well, more power to freedom, but in the process, another kind of energy has been lost—the vigor of the rolling phrase, the sonorous cadence, the flash of lyric intensity which, as in Keats, as in Shakespeare, is at time exquisite and mighty. Other, perhaps more utilitarian elements are present in current writing—but rarely is one treated to the flash of the old-fashioned electrical display.

One of the best examples of the deterioration of phrasemaking derives from the expression of patriotic sentiment. The lyric we chose for our national anthem did not shy away from what might be considered purple in today's market:

> . . . *in the twilight's last gleaming*
> . . . *gave proof through the night*
> . . . *the foe's haughty host*
> . . . *the foul footstep's pollution.*

By comparison, the hit patriotic song of the last decade was as a sparrow to an eagle, its operative lines being:

> *Stand beside her*
> *And guide her*
> *Through the night with a light from above.*

This is somewhat of a remove from

> *Mine eyes have seen the glory of the coming of the Lord*
> *He is trampling out the vintage where the grapes of wrath*
> *are stored*
> *He hath loosed the fateful lightning of His terrible swift*
> *sword:*

His truth is marching on.

The reward of a great phrase or a great lyric may not be high in ASCAP royalties or circulation, but its chance of enduring is considerable. It marches on, like truth itself, and that is no mean journey.

MEMENTO

GROUP PHOTOGRAPHS ARE, AS A RULE, STIFF
and self-conscious, and of interest to only two classes of people:
those who are in the pictures (and then only if they were
photographed well) and historians. The first may be affected
by sentimental or nostalgic associations, but to the historian
such groupings are documentary matter for the ages: They
establish who knew whom, when and where. And sometimes
they are also clues to character, as for example: Did the re-
signed president, in the photo of the graduating class of his
elementary school, already look like a person who would one
day be forced out of the biggest job in the world?

I recently came across a group photo which operates on both
sentimental and historic levels. It was of a band of admirers
who attended a party given for Carl Sandburg at the Beverly
Hilton Hotel, in the fall of 1958. Standing, left to right: Clif-
ford Odets, playwright; Robert Nathan, novelist; Ray Brad-

bury, fantasist; Dr. Joseph Kaplan, physicist; Dr. Frank Baxter, teacher; Leonard Karzmar, producer; Lion Feuchtwanger, novelist; Allan Nevins, historian; George Stevens, film director; myself, and Joe Schoenfeld, then editor of *Daily Variety*. Seated were Groucho Marx, spiffy in white tie, black beret, and a suit of youthful pattern; Georgiana Hardy, a statuesque woman prominent in Los Angeles educational circles; Sandburg, guest of honor, demurely holding a glass of scotch recumbent on his lap; and Mrs. Feuchtwanger.

The photograph brought back a swarm of memories of Sandburg, who, more than any other ranking poet in American history, was a multimedia man. He had been a newspaper reporter; he wrote poems, biographies, essays, polemics; made recordings; appeared on radio and television; played the guitar, sang folk songs; participated in panels, mixed it up in comedy shows; was a narrator for symphony orchestras (Copland's *Lincoln Portrait*); acted (the role of the prophet Jeremiah, in 1961); served as consultant on a film at 20th Century-Fox, where he occupied the absent Marilyn Monroe's bungalow; was the subject of a Broadway play (*The World of Carl Sandburg*); and, at the age of 70, finished a 1,067-page novel named *Remembrance Rock*. (He also addressed both houses of Congress, but any national hero, like the first man who walked on the moon, can do that.)

Never one to mince, Sandburg in his novel filled a mural that stretched from sea to shining sea. It was a cavalcade of characters, all interlocked with American history. Not just a pie-shaped wedge of history, but 350 years of it. The writing is solid saga—rich, patriotic and purposive, with Sandburg's gifts apparent in noble proportions, and his novelistic lacks on token display. Quite possibly it is, or will have been, the last unblushing love-of-country novel of the century. By this I mean that if one were to update the legacy placed by one of its characters under Remembrance Rock, "a handful of dust from Plymouth . . . a snuffbox filled with earth from Valley Forge . . . a little box of soil from Gettysburg . . .," not all Americans would appreciate the addition of a scrap of charcoal from Watts, a divot of turf from Santo Domingo, or a clod of mud from Tonkin Bay.

But if singing patriots with Sandburg's strength of prose are hard to come by these days, even more scarce are troubadours with his kind of voice and speech. Sandburg was forgiveably proud of his voice, and he played it better than his guitar. He used it as a musical instrument—his *ff*s were wondrous, his *pp*s were not only wondrous but occasionally inaudible. "I go very low toned at times," he once told a television producer, who replied, "We have expert engineers who will be sure to pick up every nuance of your vocal cords."

There were many nuances. Unlike most poets who read their own work, Sandburg had style, command, and, in the best sense, showmanship. He caressed vowels like an Italian, crooned with cause over certain passages, and whispered low tones when, in his unique view, the score called for them. There were also growls and sudden, explosive, haranguing shouts, and now and then a snarl of contempt, always starting on a high note and falling away in a sort of trombone slide of irony. And then he had a vein of mysticism—hushed, lyrical and sensual.

At his mystical best, he gave the impression of having confidential access to the minutes of the universe. But through all this range of delivery, Sandburg never seemed to be grandstanding. His conversation was usually as mellifluous and dramatic as his readings, so that although he was full of effects, one never felt that he did anything *for* effect. He read

intuitively, not calculatingly. Never did he mark a script for
stress or cadence or phrasing; the very idea would have offended him.

There was a well-developed fun side to Sandburg. Addiction to puns, a doting fondness for certain anecdotes, a child-
like delight in inventing creatures (hongdorshes, hoomadooms,
onkadonks and the like), a flair for comic as well as biting
parables, a genius for funnyisms that never descended to gags,
and occasional happy little observations like those about the
fingers of us all:

> Crook one finger and all the other fingers want to crook.
> Bend one finger back and all the other fingers watch what
>   happens.
> Sometimes the fingers feel sorry the thumb is not a finger.
> Look close at your thumb and you see it is not proud.
> The fingers have two knuckles, the thumb only one knuckle,
>   and they need each other.

When something struck Sandburg funny, there was no built-
in laughmeter computing whether to smile, chuckle or chortle.
He bellowed—a great, roaring laugh, his small eyes asquint
and his ample mouth wide open, like an infant bird at feeding
time, to release all that humor.

His interests, curiosity and prejudices were boundless. I
once clocked him in the course of an intended work conference with a producer—a meeting that was to have blocked out
a script for one of Sandburg's guest appearances on a network
program. Within two hours, he sang 12 songs, recited from
memory seven poems, recalled a cowboy in a rodeo in Duluth,
spoke of a blind black guitar player in Florida, digressed on
the English taste for warm beer, condemned commercialization
on TV, castigated cigarette advertising ("It's infamous the way

they indoctrinate the young people, the young people being
not aware"), glossed over nuclear weapons, Milton Berle and
Fred Allen, praised an old friend in Chicago, dismissed *Reader's Digest,* corrected a misstatement of fact about Ed Murrow's birthplace, alluded to Ezra Pound ("I'll read the sonofabitch as long as I live"), told a poignant story about Ralph
Waldo Emerson, touched on genetics, delphiniums, goats,
David Ben-Gurion, the president of Iceland, Nehru, Eisenhower ("Ike still don't know whether I write arithmetics or
geographics"), dilated on the chances for the survival of humanity, spoke ominously of China's nuclear potential, rated
Albert Schweitzer not much higher than Elvis Presley ("A
medieval theologian. I got it all in the Swedish Lutheran
Church"), and touched briefly on my collection of minerals.

There was a sense of horseplay about Sandburg that was
unexpected in a poet who could sound the deep profundities.
He once wrote me, in a postscript to a long letter, about a visit
he had from the composer Earl Robinson. During a "front-room luncheon of plain proletarian baked beans with a classy
divertissement of goat's milk," Robinson was telling Sandburg
how hard it had been to locate a certain kind of banjo:

> *He goes on how it's an old-timer with five strings and all
> Manhattan and the Atlantic seaboard didn't have any
> one could play it and you had to send to Alabama for a
> melodious galoot who knew how. Comes out then Erll
> has been on the lookout for such a banjo and had no
> luck. So yrs truly reaches over, tipping back in his chair,
> into a corner behind two guitars and a Filipino three-string fiddle and produces a banjo tt yrs truly has had
> going on 30 yrs, not playing it for 20 yrs because a guitar
> had priority. So he hands this identical banjo to Erll
> with a brief and pointed speech: "You are the one man*

in the USA to have this and I give it to you quoting the
Cossack proverb: He owns the wild horse who can ride
him." So we wrap it in a burlap bag, nickel plated with
a tight drum, long narrow fretboard, a honey. Nobody
else could have taken it away like that. It was like a good
deacon giving away an adopted child, that had always
been well behaved, to another good deacon who pledged
to bring it up well behaved and godly.

The postscript was nearing the bottom of the sheet on which
it was written, and Sandburg had room for one more sentence.
It was a media-oriented, non-sequitur sentence typical of the
irrespressible jinks in Carl's spirit:

We are returning you now to our studios and the next
voice you hear will be next voice you hear will be next
voice you hear will be—goddam that transcription!

TRUTH AS
A FRACTION

EVERY NOW AND THEN, A WRITER OR DIRECTOR comes along and knowingly fuddles the story of some great person or historical event. Ken Russell, film director, is a master of this practice. He has brought to the screen some of the glossiest garbage ever produced in the name of biographical drama, and done it with flair and sovereign arrogance. He is not one to stint on the quality of elected victims. To date Tchaikovsky, Mahler and Liszt have been brushed by his roc's wing, to the distress of their memories. I shudder to think of an indefinitely extended gallery of such portraits.

Of course Russell is entitled to his fantasies; the trouble is, he spins them around people whose lives have been well and truly documented. Let him rather work over legendary or obscure figures, like Ulysses, Tutankhamen or Theseus. With them he can doodle to his heart's content, for few can gainsay him.

Not long ago I picked up an early book by Howard Fast, entitled *Conceived in Liberty.* In it Alexander Hamilton, as aide to Washington at Valley Forge, is called on to defend three mutinous soldiers who are on trial for their lives before a court martial presided over by Generals Anthony Wayne, Nathanael Greene and Washington himself. Hamilton is valiant and eloquent, but the mutineers are found guilty and sentenced to die on the gallows. Unwilling to accept the verdict, Hamilton goes to see Washington after hours, and takes with him one of the prisoners. He pleads for a reprieve, but the expectant Father of his Country is adamant, and imperiously orders Hamilton and his charge to leave, whereupon "Hamilton dropped his head. He spoke softly. 'I wish to resign my commission. I no longer have a place here.' " Washington goes into a rage which is described as "awful and terrible," but suddenly his fury subsides, and he asks unbelievingly, "Resign your commission?"

Hamilton: "I don't want to leave, sir. Believe me, as sure as there is a God in heaven, I don't want to leave you, sir. After I leave you, there is no reason for me to live. Sir, I have no other reason to live than you and our cause."

Washington stretches out a hand and asks plaintively, "You won't leave me?" Then comes a noble speech by Hamilton: "Sir, if one life is taken unjustly . . . then a cause is dishonored. The cause exists no longer. Men can suffer for it no longer. It marks the limit of all suffering. . . ."

Technically the scene from which this fragment is taken is respectably written, just as Russell's scenes are handsomely filmed. But it is heavy with twaddle. In such recipes, half-truths are whipped into a meringue, always in the interests of "drama," as though the whole truth were not dramatic enough. The facts are these: Yes, Washington was capable of great rages; yes, Hamilton did once threaten to resign his commission; yes, Washington was reluctant to lose Hamilton because he had an almost paternal attachment to him, and leaned on him in many ways. But unlike the Fast version, Hamilton's offer to resign was actually based on personal pique, and not on lofty principle in protesting the execution of three morally innocent soldiers. (No such trial took place.) What happened was that Hamilton once offended Washington by keeping him waiting while he (Hamilton) dawdled; and when Washington calmly and civilly reproved him for this, Hamilton was so annoyed that he wanted out.

Moreover Hamilton's sanctimonious speech about having no other reason to live than Washington and "our cause," and his humanitarian outcry against the unjust taking of life, are at deep variance with the record of his attitudes and character. Far from being zealous for the lives and safety of soldiers, Hamilton, in the battle of Yorktown, recklessly, needlessly and deliberately exposed a unit under his command to enemy fire. Later he did his inspired best to embroil America in a war with its recent ally, France. He was an extreme hawk who more than once insisted on solving problems by force rather than through negotiation.

So much for historical truth from an established American novelist. But television is capable of circulating half-truths and three-quarter-truths far more broadly, by a factor of millions, than any biographical novel could possibly do. An abridged TV version of the Lincoln-Douglas debates, based on a stage play which was at pains to stick to history, canceled many of those pains and presented a Douglas altered to conform to a director's concept of Douglas, and to hell with Burgundy.

As in so many other precincts of esthetics, questions like those of license come down finally to a matter of degree. A first-

rate documentary film, *I Will Fight No More Forever,* dealt
with the Nez Percé Indians and their struggle against an oppressive campaign by the government to chase them off their
land. The program was prefaced by a title claiming the story
was true, and this quiet claim, intended to serve in a general
way, became the subject of a thoughtful essay by Michael J.
Arlen in *The New Yorker.* In it Arlen, while admiring the
program, cited discrepancies from the archives. "Some are
minor," he acknowledged, "and of what might be called a
technical or pedantic nature . . . some inaccuracies are inci-
dental in terms of telling a dramatic story, others are a result
of the unscriptability of nature."

Had Arlen himself worked in TV and films, he would have
known that in any well-intentioned and truth-seeking documentary, much besides nature is unscriptable, and sometimes
minor license must be taken with respect to time, place and
atmosphere. So long as such liberties are small and rational,
they are acceptable divergences, and may in good conscience
be taken. Thus *I Will Fight No More* kept its integrity in
spite of a few functional discrepancies from truth. The technical and pedantic are of little concern; what is important is the
main design, the sweep and the spirit. If these are true to history, the rest is peanuts, relatively speaking.

Historical and biographical drama does not necessarily demand unyielding fidelity to fact, nor does it impose the kind of
strictures that are drawn by lawyers. The overliteral can become the underachieved in dramatic effect, and there is no
excuse, not even a note from mother, for dullness. Indeed
license is the birthright, if not the obligation, of every art.
Without it, the mysterious afflatus we call imagination would
have no place to call home. Nevertheless dramatic and poetic
license are subject to a certain decorum when in the presence

of established record. It is proper for yeasty fantasy to rise in *Alice in Wonderland,* but the same fermentation would be amiss in a biography of Lewis Carroll.

Documentary dramatists are obliged to do right by persons and events in all matters of substance and consequence. If major fractions of truth are discounted, if there is distortion or concealment or misrepresentation or Russelline self-indulgence, what comes out is a nonstatutory form of perjury. Dean Swift, back in 1726, had Lemuel Gulliver complain that he was "chiefly disgusted with modern history. For having strictly examined all the persons of greatest name for an hundred years past, I found how the world had been misled by prostitute writers." Had TV and films existed on Glubbdubdrib, Gulliver might have added directors and producers.

The more remote the epoch, and the more undocumented the background and principal characters, the greater the freedom to speculate. Shakespeare exercised the broadest license with his kings, with Caesar and Brutus, Anthony and Cleopatra. But had Caesar left tapes behind, had Brutus left as many letters as Jefferson did, had Cleopatra written a daily column like Eleanor Roosevelt, and had the Roman Bureau of Public Archives printed every last speech of Marc Antony, it would have been impossible for Shakespeare to have dealt with these notables quite as he did.

It is often argued that so long as a historical presentation is entertaining, anything goes, and all excesses are to be forgiven. On Gore Vidal's *Burr,* critics were so divided over the novel's fractional truths and frettings of fancy that in the columns of the august *New York Times Book Review,* one of the editors took out after a reviewer who, in the same journal, had earlier quarreled with Vidal's easy-going approach to that old-time religion of verity.

The sacrifice of truth for what is loosely called entertainment, becomes, at times, like sacrificing a child to satisfy some hungry god. There is usually wonder and drama and power enough in the whole truth without having to garnish the spread. To me a scene in which Alexander Hamilton haughtily offers to pull out because George Washington properly scolded him for being late, is just as dramatic as a fabrication in which Hamilton wants to quit over a verdict. The former may be even more dramatic since it affords us a glimpse into the true character of a man whose life and work stand among our national monuments.

"Nothing is poetical if plain daylight is not poetical," wrote Chesterton, "and no monster should amaze us if the normal man does not amaze." Right, G. K. Neither truth, nor pills nor lilies need to be gilded. "Wasteful and ridiculous excess," is what our man in Stratford called it.

IMPERISHABLE SPANIARD

ANOTHER BOOK AND A NEW PLAY ON THE LIFE
of Miguel de Cervantes have appeared, giving further evidence
that the media, praise the Lord, will never be finished with the
man and his work, any more than Verdi will ever drop out of
the repertoire of opera, or Shakespeare vanish from stage or
screen.

If you look into the life and times of Cervantes, you will be
struck by the parallels and divergences between him and
Shakespeare. They happened to be contemporaries, and died
in the same year. Some say on the same day, and offer elaborate
proofs to this effect. But there is no evidence that either of
them ever read the work of the other, nor that they knew of
each other's existence. This may be sad for sentimental and
other considerations, but one hardly need strain for a reason.
England and Spain were then in no mood for cultural ex-

change. They were fiercely antagonistic, and their period of intensest enmity cut across the prime of both men's lives.

The Spanish Armada, for whose provision Cervantes worked as a commissary, was called Invincible by everybody in Spain. It was fattened and groomed to attack the Britain of Elizabeth, and there was no question in the mind of anybody around Madrid that the squadrons of Philip II would sweep everything before them. Instead, thanks to British seamanship, Atlantic gales and the ineptness of the Spanish command, the Armada was destroyed, and with it, Spanish power. Heavy gloom descended on the already bleak Escorial, and on its royal tenant, who was apparently born morose.

In England, on the other hand, there was an upwelling of vigor. Not surprisingly, in the historical canvases that Shakespeare was soon to create, there would be little of modest proportion. His plays do not lack for panache and bravado; a spirit of grandeur and nobility invests them all. Shakespeare was sure of his materials, sure that his plays would be performed, sure of approbation.

Cervantes was sure of nothing. Not even of whether he could earn enough money to be solvent. Not even sure he could stay out of prison. Up through his late fifties he was, by all ordinary standards, a failure. He had written a conventional, posturing pastoral novel, some hack poetry, a grandiose historical drama and a few plays which were driven out of the market by a steady tattoo of popular works from the tireless hand of Lope de Vega.

So when Cervantes began writing *The Ingenious Gentleman Don Quixote de la Mancha*, his stance was as far removed from that of Shakespeare embarking on, let's say, *Macbeth*, as Pluto flies distant from Mercury. Instead of fanfares, flourishes and big entrances, Cervantes' hero, a batty old man, starts out alone on a grandly irrational pursuit. Only as an afterthought is Sancho Panza, one of the most delightful characters in all literature, introduced. Cervantes had to bring Quixote back and start out all over again, because it became clear that the Don needed a foil; that it would be too difficult a business for Cervantes to have the Knight go it alone.

The adventures begin without the slightest expectation by the author that they will broaden and compound into a masterpiece of vast dimension. By the time Quixote comes home to die, a thousand pages along, he and Sancho have been joined in the story by 997 other characters. And enough fuel has been produced not only to keep the universal reader warmed and entertained, but to keep the wheels of Media spinning eternally.

Consider the forms in which Quixote has already been recreated, beyond effigies, cheap souvenirs and statuary: there are plays, operas, ballets, tone poems, musical comedies, television specials, paintings, etchings and motion pictures. The Russians made a movie starring Chaliapin. The Americans made a movie miscasting Peter O'Toole. Television came up with a 90-minute version miscasting Rex Harrison. Richard Strauss wrote a symphonic work. Maurice Ravel wrote songs. The Hollywood Bowl, in the summer of 1973, gave a concert of works based on Quixote, including Strauss, Telemann, Massenet and Ibert. Gustave Dore created an album of Quixote illustrations which is a joy to the world. Daumier did a painting on Quixote and Sancho. Goya and Fragonard did drawings. Scores of lesser masters, like Bonington and Vanderbank, have done variations. The actor Richard Kiley became indelibly identified with both Cervantes and Quixote. Thomas Mann wrote a monumental essay. And so on and on.

To the dramatist, painter, composer and producer, *Don*

Quixote is an inexhaustible mine. The tilting against the windmill, the helmet of Mambrino, the wine-spilling episode, the liberation of the convicts, the disruption of the funeral procession, the annihilation of the puppets—all these have been exploited in various versions on the stage and screen. With respect to Dulcinea del Toboso, the great lady who exists only in Quixote's imagination, most of the dramatists and librettists have made a romantic fabrication of her that completely ignores the wonderfully tongue-in-cheek satire of Cervantes. In *Man of La Mancha*, Dulcinea materialized as a prostitute in the very earthy shape of Sophia Loren; in the Rex Harrison television version, she was an elegant, entirely corporeal lady, with no blemish whatever on her escutcheon.

But there are many more episodes in *Quixote* that have never been approached, especially events in Part II, the sequel to the first volume, which Cervantes completed after an interval of 10 years. One such is the occasion of Quixote's lordly advice to Sancho when the latter, through an elaborate joke, is about to become Governor of Barataria. The speech, a long one, is wonderfully droll, pompous and, at the same time, infused with wisdom. It resembles the advice of Polonius to Laertes in *Hamlet*, except that Cervantes cannot resist the urge to be funny, as in a passage about the impropriety of a governor belching in public. Among nuggets of advice:

> *Walk slowly, but not in such a manner as to give the impression that you are listening to yourself.*

Concerning Sancho's lack of qualifications for the job, Quixote says:

> *We know from long experience that neither much ability nor much learning is necessary in order to be a governor.*

The Ingenious Gentleman, being immortal, has fresh things to say to succeeding generations and cultural epochs. To the seventeenth and eighteenth centuries, the woeful knight appeared mainly as a comical and at times slapstick figure, jouncing and jousting through a broad satire on the romances of chivalry. The nineteenth century found deeper implications in the conflict between idealism and pragmatism. Our own century has added to all this an awareness of profound insights into the nature of madness, the dualism of body and soul, the reciprocal interplay between the individual and society.

As for Cervantes himself, it is ironic that so few hard facts are known about a man who wrote so much. *Don Quixote* was not his only credit, as we say today. He also turned out a pastoral novel, *Galatea,* the plays and the historical epic mentioned earlier, plus a batch of sonnets, letters in verse, and odes, including one on kidney diseases. There were also some late short stories, which he grouped under the heading of *Exemplary Novels.*

The chief clues to the curricula vitae of his life, to his travels, activities and associations, come through meager official documents, registrations, court orders and the like; the rest must be extrapolated from what are assumed to be autobiographical elements in *Don Quixote* and the *Exemplary Novels.* The crowning irony is that nobody today even knows where Cervantes is buried—he, author of the second most widely published and translated book in the world. (First is the Bible.) Not bad for a man who was considered a hack writer for most of his 69 years.

LYRICS, YEAH

QUESTION: WHO WROTE THE LYRICS OF THE best known song of indigence in American history, *Brother Can You Spare a Dime?* He also wrote the words for the score of *The Wizard of Oz*, including the hit which Judy Garland endowed with life eternal—*Somewhere Over the Rainbow;* and he was author of *How Are Things in Glocca Morra*, among other tasty canapés in *Finian's Rainbow*, including but not limited to the plaintively blithe lines of a leprechaun troubled by fickleness in love:

> *When I can't fondle the hand I'm fond of,*
> *I'll fondle the hand at hand ...*
> *When I'm not near the girl I love,*
> *I love the girl I'm near.*
> > *What if they're tall or tender,*
> > *What if they're small or slender,*
> > *As long as they've got that gender*
> *I surrender.*

These, as well as the lyrics for *Bloomer Girl, Cabin in the Sky* and the even more familiar *April in Paris,* were written by E. Y. Harburg, better known by his nickname Yip. One might call him the grand old man of American lyricists, were it not for the impertinence of the second adjective. Grand he certainly is, but although he is into his 80's, he cannot be described as old. He demonstrated this not long ago, in the course of a lecture to a university class of songwriters, when he took on new practitioners with an outspokenness authorized by his many credits and lofty ASCAP rating.

"Lyrics have no roots today," he charged, in a ventilation of scorn hitherto unpublished. "Songs to me were stardust. Today they're sawdust. They are the songs of the people who lack roots, who don't know where they are. They're yearning, they're searching for somewhere to go. But no one knows where he wants to go unless he knows where he's been, and how he came about.

"If you're a lyric writer and you don't know who Herrick is, or Suckling or Wordsworth or Dorothy Parker or Franklin P. Adams—if you don't know versification, how to write rhymes, what the discipline of rhyming is, how can you write lyrics? We're in an age of instancy—instant coffee, instant cake mix, instant beauty and instant songs—and that's what they sound like. If you're out to make money, to make a hit, fine—but if you want to be a Cole Porter, Ira Gershwin, Johnny Mercer, a Noël Coward, (a lot of the songs they wrote 50 years ago are still hanging in there, and are the basis of the ASCAP catalogue), if you want your songs to *last,* if you want to be an artist and not a hack, then you must ask yourself whether you are writing for the quick buck, or because you believe songwriting is an important and powerful method of communicating with people."

Harburg went on to claim for the popular song an ubiqui-
tousness usually ascribed only to taxes and inflation, when he
spoke of songs following us wherever we go—"in your eleva-
tor, in your dentist's chair, in your shopping center; and
whether you know it or not, you and your children are listening to *words*, to *language*, which is the tool of communication.
You (songwriters) can demote intelligence, you can help ruin
the language of a country with stuff like, 'Yeah, baby; dig it,
man; you know; I mean; like.' The songs I hear today have no
discipline, no rhyme; they're reportage, they're mundane; they
have no twinkle, no humor. You are writing songs of genocide,
suicide—you left me, baby, yeah; I left you; bleeding heart
songs, open surgery songs, shorthand songs, dementia praecox
music, gibberish, no roots, yeah, yeah. It's got to have roots.
You've got to know what a good phrase is, and what a bad
phrase is."

Any artist who openly criticizes others in his same craft runs
the standard risk of the occupant of a glass house who throws
stones. But in Harburg's case, he has license to tick off the
particulars of his indictment, since he has never himself been
guilty of the crimes and misdemeanors he alluded to. His
lyrics have been responsible. They have rhyme, twinkle, good
phrasing, discipline, and humor. Though he communicates
ideas and supports causes, he is never arch or formal, forensic
or didactic. He makes no secret of his liberal-progressive stance,
of a sweeping humanism that has occasionally earned him the
displeasure of establishment authorities and rednecks. Although he sometimes uses satire as a weapon, he wields it
gently; he is not out to kill but to persuade through emotion,
to appeal to both head and heart, to do what he considers the
obligation of songwriters—to communicate. A good example
was in a show that came ahead of its time as an expression of

women's rights—*Bloomer Girl*. In the book of this musical, a
runaway slave is reproached by his master: "I don't understand
you. Ain't I always treat you well when you were sick? Given
you food? Been a big brother to you?"

"Yes, Boss," answers the slave. "But with all that food
and warmth, there was a sickness I had—every time I heard
that railroad whistle going by at night, I'd get sick at the
stomach. I wanted to be on that train." And then he sings a
song with typical Harburg lyrics—loose, sweet, easy, and full
of spirit. The chorus goes:

> *River it like to flow*
> *Eagle it like to fly*
> *Eagle it like to feel its wings*
> *Against the sky*
> *Possum it like to run*
> *Ivy it like to climb*
> *Bird in the tree*
> *And bumblebee*
> *Want freedom. . . .*
>
> *Free as the sun is free*
> *That's how it's gotta be*
> *Whatever is right for bumblebee and river and eagle*
> *Is right for me.*
> *We gotta be free*
> *The eagle and me.*

With Harburg's *J'Accuse* in mind, I checked, at random,
some of the lyrics of the Beatles, Jethro Tull, The Beach
Boys, Buffalo Springfield, Queen, Al Stewart, Elton John,
King Crimson, Stevie Wonder. I found plenty of yeahs, yehs
and yeas. Obviously Yes is a square word in these circles.

She's got soul, yeah
It's up to you, yeah
Whenever I want you around, yeh
Pretty black beauty, yeah, yea, yeah,
Yeah, yeah, all right, ah ha
She loves you, yeh, hey hey
You're a bluebird, yea—yea, yea
beep, beep, mm, beep, beep, yeh

The plank on "instancy" was confirmed by the Beatles in discussions of the way their songs came about:

"We were sitting in the studio and made it up out of thin air"; "There's a lot of random in our songs"; "I was doodling"; "I was bopping about on the piano"; "Paul said we should do a real song in the studio. Could I whip one off?"; "I was just thinking of nice words like Sergeant Pepper and Lonely Hearts Club, and they came together for no reason."

Sins against rhyme strew the songscape with such unhappy partnerships of non-rhyme as farm and phone, leaving and pleasing, trains and laid, died and survive, surgery and successfully, El Paso and hassle.

Crude and sloppy phrases are commoner even than yeahs:

Just as hate knows love's the cure
You can rest your mind assure [sic]
That I'll be loving you always

and

Now you relax and let your mind go free,
You won't regret the feeling you receive.

another:

I'll cop out to the change,
But a stranger is putting the tease on . . .

> *Stick around while the clown who is sick*
> *Does the trick of disaster*
> *For the race of my head and my face is moving faster.*

For mixed metaphors, few lyrics can challenge

> *So hard to shed the life of before,*
> *To let my soul automatically soar*
> *But I hit hard at the battle that confronts me.*

and again

> *A diamond necklace, played the pawn,*
> *Hand in hand some drummed along,*
> *To a handsome man and baton.*
> *A blind aristocracy,*
> *Back through the op'ra glass you see*
> *The pit and the pendulum drawn . . .*

Often, as in the last two, allusions are so private or obscure as to be meaningless except to the author, and perhaps even to him.

> *I'm going up the "Pool"*
> *From down the Smoke below*
> *To taste me mum's jam "Sarnis"*
> *And see our Aunty Flo*

The alienation of which Harburg spoke is present over a broad range of lyrics:

> *Unfeeling, feel lonely rejection,*
> *Unknowing, you're going wrong*

> *We were talking about the space between us all*
> *And the people who hide themselves behind a wall*

Out of my mind and I just can't take it anymore . . .
Left behind by myself and what I'm living for.
All I hear are screams
From outside the limousines
That are taking me out of my mind.

The inarticulateness that hobbles so many young songsmiths
is not from shyness but poverty of language. Just as "real" and
"neat" have become lazy all-purpose words of approbation, so
"all right" has moved into prominence as a statement of karma,
gestalt, quality of life, or temporary condition:

Whatever gets them through the night,
'Sallright, 'sallright.

I'll buy you a diamond ring, my friend,
If it makes you feel all right.

When I get near you
The games begin to drag me down
It's all right.

The cult of car and motorbike have broadened the base of
modern lyrics. Here is Bernie Taupin for Elton John:

A couple of the sounds that I really like
Are the sounds of a switchblade and a motorbike.

From the Queen group:

Such a thrill when your radials squeal

Told my girl I just had to forget her
Rather buy me a new carburettor [sic]

Yet notwithstanding the yeahs and allrights and mangled

metaphors, there are still some solid virtues in the new genera-
tion of lyricists, which even Harburg would acknowledge.
There are social awareness and concern, among artists like
Stevie Wonder:

> *Families buying dog food now*
> *Starvation roams the streets*
> *Babies die before they're born*
> *Infected by the grief*

and the Beatles:

> *Lady Madonna children at your feet*
> *Wonder how you manage to make ends meet*
> *Who finds the money when you pay the rent?*
> *Lady Madonna baby at your breast*
> *Wonder how you manage to feed the rest*

and Jethro Tull:

> *Well, I tried my best to love you all,*
> *All you hypocrites and whores,*
> *With your eyes on each other*
> *And the locks upon your doors.*

And there is a fine anti-pollution song by the Beach Boys,
called *A Day in the Life of a Tree;* and the bitter *Uno Mundo,*
of Buffalo Springfield, which has "Asia screaming, Africa
seething, faithful scheming, America bleeding."

There are ordered and disciplined verses, too, and some happiness. Not even in Harburg is there anything sunnier than
the Beatles'

> *Good day sunshine, good day sunshine, good day sunshine,*
> *I need to laugh, and when the sun is out,*
> *I've got something I can laugh about.*

I feel good in a special way,
I'm in love, and it's a sunny day.

Nor is there any cheerier song than Jethro Tull's *Grace*, which is only four lines long:

Hello sun
Hello bird
Hello my lady.
Hello breakfast. May I buy you again tomorrow?

And there are occasional rhymes as playful as anything in Harburg's witty and ingratiating repertoire. Witness this fragment from a song by Al Stewart:

Love was a rollaway
Just a cajoleaway
Love was a stealaway
Just a reveal away.

So it is not all gloom and pellagra, as the opening quotations from Harburg would seem to suggest, and it would be unfair to Harburg to imply that he thinks we should write off the whole of a generation's work. But it is good for young lyricists to hear a master sound off, and be advised by a laureate as to what it takes to make a song last a long time.

Still, when it comes to posterity, Yip Harburg himself has reservations. In his book of poems, *At This Point in Time*, he asks

Why should I write for posterity?
What, if I may be free
To ask a ridiculous question,
Has posterity done for me?

Not much yet, Yip, but give it a chance.

THE FEW APPROPRIATE
REMARKS

THE GETTYSBURG ADDRESS IS SO FAMILIAR TO
so many people, that one feels almost apologetic to bring it up
again. Yet it is like a gram of radium whose energy is out of
all proportion to its size, and whose radiations are steady and
persistent.

Ten sentences, that's all. But they're a national treasure, and
one of the monuments of world history. The speech, like
Abraham Lincoln himself, long ago passed beyond the need for
praise; now it remains only to be marveled at, enjoyed for its
beauty, and cherished for its substance.

Still, new things are always being discovered about it, and
perhaps this is one: the address, and the events surrounding it,
make an almost perfect small-scale model of Lincoln and his
times. If by some unfortunate mandate it became necessary
for us to reduce volumes to paragraphs, and murals to the size
of postage stamps, one could learn enough from the Gettys-

burg episode in Lincoln's career alone, to understand a great
deal about the man, about his era, his cause and his country.

We would learn not only the obvious things—that Lincoln
had a noble cast of mind, that he was humane, that he had a
deep sense of the sanctity of life together with a compassion
for those in travail, and a touching respect for the honored
dead. But you would also learn that Lincoln was modest, hard-
working and patient; that he fussed about his writing; that he
was gracious to a point of gallantry; that he tended to run
down his own accomplishments, and had a generally pessi-
mistic view about the chances of anything he did amounting
to much or shaking the world; that Americans were capable of
being touched by his words, and were in every way worthy of
them; that there were present in the land men of such ill will
and hostility that they were violently offended by the Gettysburg Address; but there were also men of clear vision who,
within 24 hours of the occasion, reached the same estimate of
the greatness of the speech that we all concur in some 115
years later.

You may ask how Lincoln's modesty was involved. In the
first place, the program dedicating the national soldier's cemetery at Gettysburg was not built around the President at all.
He was invited as an afterthought.

The main part of the program had been arranged for almost
two months before Lincoln was asked to make "a few appropriate remarks toward the end of the exercise." The feature of the
program was to be an oration by Edward Everett, a polished
speaker who had rounded off his style and manner as a United
States Senator, a governor of Massachusetts and a president of
Harvard. Obviously the man for the job.

A vain chief executive and Commander-In-Chief of the
Armed Forces might have felt slighted to be invited late, to

find himself journeying to Gettysburg to sit on a platform for hours, listening to the speaker of the day and the Baltimore Glee Club, only to get up at the close and make a few appropriate remarks to an audience by this time tired of standing. But not Lincoln. He accepted, and went. He worked hard on his few remarks. The night before, on a train rolling toward Pennsylvania, he excused himself from some company by saying, "Gentlemen, this is all very pleasant, but the people will expect me to say something to them tomorrow, and I must give the matter some thought."

He gave it thought in the form of several drafts without the help of a ghost writer, and he kept revising the speech right up to the moment he delivered it. In fact, he made changes after he got to his feet.

Nothwithstanding all the work he had put into these ten sentences, he was not satisfied. Just after he finished making the speech, he told a friend that it wouldn't stick . . . called it a flat failure, and said he was sure people were disappointed by it. Here, Lincoln was true to his accustomed pattern. Hadn't he said, during a campaign for the Senate, that the job was too big for him? Hadn't he prophesized that he would never be president? Hadn't he announced, following his defeat for the senatorship by Douglas, that he, Lincoln, would now sink out of view and be forgotten? In the Gettysburg Address itself, he did it again . . . made a wrong prophecy about himself. "The world," he said, "will very little note nor long remember what we say here."

There were those who were only too happy to agree with him. A Pennsylvania paper dismissed his address as a series of "silly remarks" and hoped that "for the credit of the nation, the veil of oblivion shall be dropped over them. and that they be no more repeated or thought of."

The *Chicago Times* said Lincoln had "foully traduced the motives of the men slain at Gettysburg," and was deeply mortified in behalf of the country: "The cheek of every American must tingle with shame as he reads the silly, flat, and dishwatery utterances of the man who has to be pointed out to intelligent foreigners as the President of the United States."

We had that type of journalism then, as now. But others took a quite opposite view. There were those who, overnight, were able to size up Lincoln's few remarks as being appropriate for, and worthy of, the attention of posterity. A reporter for the *Chicago Tribune* wired back: "The remarks of Lincoln will live among the annals of man." The *Cincinnati Gazette* found the speech "perfect in every respect"; the *Springfield* (Massachusetts) *Republican* commended it as "worthy of study as a model speech."

The Lincoln legend has been long on his craggy humor, his sufferings and melancholy, his lofty sentiment, his kindliness, and many other attributes, but less often is there recalled his charm and graciousness. Here again, the Gettysburg occasion gives us a glowing example. Following the exercises at the cemetery, Mr. Everett, whose two-hour address had been turned out with considerable thought, wrote to Lincoln: "I should be glad if I could flatter myself that I came as near the central idea of the occasion in two hours as you did in two minutes."

What did Lincoln reply to this? What would *you* have replied to such a compliment from a speaker with whom you had shared a program? Lincoln's brief answer was as beautiful an example of tact and the return of a good word as there exists in the language:

"In our respective parts yesterday, you could not have been excused to make a short address, nor I a long one. I am pleased to know that, in your judgment, the little I did say was not entirely a failure."

So far from a failure was the little Mr. Lincoln did say, that we continue to read and speak it across the decades, enshrining it with familiarity, yet always learning from it, and doing our best, most of the time, to live up to it.

HARMLESS AFFAIRS

OCCASIONALLY IN A WEAK OR DISTRACTED
moment, I agree to participate in a panel. It was on one of
these that I discovered I was a *discussant*. That is what it said
on the printed program. I had never seen the word before, and
at first I thought it was merely another token of my pro-
vincialism, until I found that both the Webster unabridged
and the Oxford concise dictionaries had never heard of it
either, and Roget was equally dark.

As I am never one to pass up the chance to doodle over a
word when I have a thousand more urgent things to do, I pursued my research into other dictionaries, and at last I was rewarded. It is in the Random House unabridged.

I was uneasy about my billing as a discussant, because the
suffix "-ant" makes a kind of insectant out of almost everything
it touches. Like sycophant or mendicant or supplicant. The
ant-words in general lack a certain élan, they lack nobility,

they seem not to be working for any good cause. Take, for example, expectorant. And pollutant. And dependant. And defendant. And servant. The only one of the ant-words that has any grandeur to speak of is elephant, and that would disappear as soon as the meaning were changed to one who elephs.

I think every one of us should have an affair, or at least a series of flirtations, with the language into which we were born. Not necessarily a serious affair, leading to a permanent arrangement like a career in etymology or linguistics, but a fling, a trip, a romp. There have been occasional attempts by the media to make recreation of words, and I will come to this, but perhaps first I should define the kind of divertissement I have in mind.

Let us take, for a random starter, the curious affinity of words beginning with "sn" for functions and expressions of the head and its parts—especially the nose, mouth and throat. At first this sounds ludicrous, but read on.

A disparaging term for the nose is snout. When the snout tickles, you sneeze. Or perhaps you sniffle. The sniffle is of course descended from the sniff. A leading sniffable substance, much safer than glue to inhale, is snuff. Usually followed by a sneeze. Enough sniffling, snuffing and sneezing, and you may be ready for a snooze. During which you may snore. On awakening you may be hungry enough to want a snack, and may find yourself snooping around the kitchen. If no snack is to be had, you may snort with frustration or snarl on general principles.

It is with the head, and no other member of the body, that we are snippy, that we snitch on or snub someone, that we may be snide, that we snicker or snivel or snuffle or sneer. It is around the hair of the head that a snood is worn.

The "sn" combination applies also to accessories of the nose and mouth. The breathing apparatus of a submerged submarine (or a submerged human, for that matter) is a snorkel. And the bridle bit, or mouthpiece of a horse, is called a snaffle. A supercilious snob, whose snub nose is in the air, may be, and has been, described as snotty.

There could well be some relationship of the "sn" syndrome to the term "snow" for cocaine or heroin, as sniffed by addicts. Possibly it is called snow for its appearance—but if that is the case, why aren't sugar and salt and flour or any other white powder called snow?

The Scotch dialect word for sniff is snook, but one doesn't have to go to Scotland to be understood when you "cock a snook" at someone. It means to thumb one's nose. And insolent talk, which after all issues from the mouth, is called snash. The latter is another Scotticism, but it is expressive enough to belong to us all.

Almost as though a little envious of the "sn" association, "sm" hovers about the head too. As in smell and smooch. And smile and smirk and smack. And smarmy. Smoking is a candidate, but many other things besides tobacco and grass are smoked—like hams and eels and whitefish—so the nose-mouth-head axis cannot claim smoke in the same way it includes smothering.

M tries hard, but it does not make out as well as N, in the context of the human head. Even though M has the distinction of beginning mouth and muzzle, as well as all those sotto voce sounds like mutter and murmur and mumble. Above the mouth is the moustache; the face as a whole is a mug. One masticates or munches with the help of molars. To be voiceless is to be mute or mum.

Still, N wins going away. Not only for its collaborative services in the "sn" vocabulary, but for straight-out head identifications such as noggin, nut, nozzle, nip, nag, nod, nostrils, noddle, neck, nape, nib, nibble, nosh (now officially appropriated from Yiddish), nuzzle and, for any horses who may be reading this, neigh.

I could go on for another five pages, but by then the affair might get out of hand. The point is that the peculiarities of language are a source of innocent merriment; at least a pleasant way to pass time; at most (and in this case most is a good deal) an excellent way to interest youngsters in language. Ask *Sesame Street*. Or better, watch it.

Word play is a little like being turned loose at a table of palate-tickling hors d'oeuvres. It is not a meal, but man does not live by entrées alone. The media have made occasional passes at these delights. As critics say of works they admire but which they feel may not have general appeal, word pleasure is not for everyone. Radio, television and publication have had their innings, and their success has been steady but modest. CBS once had a radio program called *We Take Your Word*. Sidney J. Harris, a widely syndicated columnist, every now and then succumbs:

> *All right, I give in. When the letter-basket labelled "Language" reaches a certain height, I know it's time to do another column on words.*

Jack Smith, of whose world I am a happy citizen, serves a tray of superior antipasto when the mood is upon him, as it was when he wrote on malapropisms, especially misheard phrases like "Lead us not into Penn Station," and "Hollywood be thy name." He invented some first-rate ones of his own:

> *She retarded and moved to Laguna to live on her pen-*
> *chant and her diffidence. . . .*

Archie Bunker got off somewhat studied malapropisms in
"All in the Family"; they were good but uneven, because they
came from an assortment of writers, but they were still entertaining, and were part of Archie's perverse charm.

James Lipton's book, *An Exaltation of Larks,* is the definitive
funland of collective nouns (a pride of lions, a gam of whales,
a shrivel of critics, an odium of politicians, an acne of adoles-
cents).

Periodicals contribute. Ray Bongartz in the *Saturday Re-*
view (" 'I'm Dying', He Croaked") created a landmark of its
kind.

Among the many serious works—serious in the sense of
their scope, not in any absence of wit—are the books of Mario
Pei and Charlton Laird. For etymology, one can hardly improve on Joseph T. Shipley's *Dictionary of Word Origins* for
a light touch embroidering sound scholarship. Eric Partridge's
Short Etymological Dictionary of Modern English Origins is,
like its title, not very short (970 pages) and is as sober as a
bishop facing excommunication. It is exhaustive and valuable,
and apparently does not have time for the kind of play that
Shipley and Smith and a legion of us enjoy.

Partridge, preceding his foreword, quotes the poet William
Cowper:

> *Philologists who chase*
> *A panting syllable through time and space,*
> *Start it at home, and hunt it in the dark,*
> *To Gaul, to Greece, and into Noah's Ark.*

Which brings me to a comic strip named *Boner's Ark,* drawn

by one Addison (first name unsigned) and distributed by King Features. Boner, a simple fellow who captains an ark full of animals, calls his passengers together and reads an order. Standing around listening are snakes, birds, simians, elephants, hippos, a mule and several unidentifiable species. Boner speaks:

> *Out of respect for our fellow passengers, the following expressions are now taboo: I'm a monkey's uncle, You dirty rat, Stubborn as a mule, Dumb bunny, It's for the birds, You bug me, Drunk as a skunk, You lowdown snake, I could eat a horse, Stool-pigeon, Chicken-hearted, Dead as a dodo, Eat crow, Shoot the bull, Gone ape, Crazy as a loon, It's a dog's life, Slothful, and Batty.*

An elephant, standing toward the rear of the assembly, agrees with the proscription. "It's *time* they stopped talking about us like that!" he trumpets. But a mule, wearing only a collar, tie and a plaintive expression, demurs. "Gee," he says, "I've always liked the publicity."

MAILBOX ON MARS

THOUSANDS OF SCIENTISTS, ENGINEERS AND workers contributed to the marvel of playing migs 250 million miles across space, and plunking an aggie onto a target on the surface of Mars. Add to these thousands, another three billion humans who swarm on this, our bigger-sister planet, and then stand back and contemplate the number. Yet out of all these teeming Malthusian hordes, out of all the nations with their glittering hardware, their launching pads, their solemn savants and cabinets, their Congresses, standing armies, interlocking directorates, conventions, postal systems bearing Amazonian floods of mail every day, out of the trillions of words spoken into instruments and naked ears; out of masses of humanity so huge that God is said to be considering a new Commandment, *Thou Shalt Plan Thy Family Before Thee*, out of this whole fantastic pool of vast statistics, there is only one man— one name—that readers associate emotionally with the greatest of explorations into the unknown. He is an American, born in Illinois and domiciled in California.

In July of the year of our Bicentennial, a cartoon by Frank Interlandi was carried by a national newspaper syndicate. It depicted a bleak landscape on Mars as we have come to know it in closeup, thanks to our Viking messenger. The scene is desolate except for one feature standing sharp and clear: a mailbox. The name on the box is Ray Bradbury.

When the Viking, after its incredible journey, touched down like a ballerina's foot on the face of Mars, and the first thrilling photographs began to thread their beads of light and shadow back to earth, who do you suppose was at the Jet Propulsion Laboratory in Pasadena, drinking champagne with the management and crew? And who did people congratulate for weeks afterward, as though he himself had planned and executed the whole show?

And what has Bradbury done that his name comes ahead even of his country's in our consciousness of Mars? Did he drive a space ship into some dazzling quadrant of the zodiac, like those astronauts and cosmonauts whose names are beginning to slip from easy memory? Bradbury doesn't even drive an automobile. Was he a passenger, then, on some glamorous cosmic shot? He has never even been a passenger on a commercial or any other kind of airplane. Airplanes scare him.

What *did* he do, then? Well, all he did was write. He is an artist, and he got to Mars before the scientists. Long before. His words, his *Martian Chronicles*, the beauty and vibrance of his imagery, his imagination, carried us to a Mars that theretofore had been only a cold body of astronomical statistics and inconclusive telescopic observations. No matter that Ray's landscapes were richer than what the Viking looked around and saw. No matter that there are no somber cities on Mars, nor any ectoplasmic populations. Mars was, to the best of man's intents and purposes, captured by Ray Bradbury. He colonized it with his poetry. No amount of scientific data, no logs and extrapolations of computer codes, will ever dislodge him from that planet. His mailbox, like those first firm footprints on the moon, will stand there forever.

Now the writing of science fiction is an honorable activity of wide scope, and its finest practitioners, like H. G. Wells, Olaf Stapledon, C. S. Lewis, Robert Heinlein, William F. Nolan, Kurt Vonnegut, are justly famed. But to describe Bradbury as a science fiction writer is like describing a steam locomotive as a vehicle without indicating how big it is, how many wheels it has, what weight it pulls, how fast it goes, how wonderful is its plume of smoke and what a majestic thunder it makes.

Bradbury writes science fiction all right, but he also writes poems and short stories and stage plays and screenplays and radio plays and essays and articles and character studies and polemics, and, God knows, letters that have the same color and vitality as the rest of his writing and himself. He is a man of extraordinary dimensions; he has a contagious élan which sets him apart from the world-weary, effete, cynical, success-spoiled, profit-struck or neurasthenic among his brethren. More than any other man I know, he is an evangelist of art, and the art he cares about most is writing. For though he gives abundant honor to space men and scientists, he reserves his most ardent offices for the dignity and craft of the writer. One has only to read his marvelously elliptical yet heartfelt tributes to Charles Dickens, Emily Dickinson, Herman Melville, Gerard Manley Hopkins, Thomas Wolfe and Ernest Hemingway, to confirm this.

In a sense Bradbury is a missionary not only for art, but for life. He is an affirmationist. I have seen him angry at times, I have seen him excited, but never gloomy, never remorseful, never despairing. He swigs the elixirs of existence, and passes them around, not only in print but in person.

Happily for him, he is honored in his own time and country. What more approbation can there be for a writer than to appear in the main vocabulary of dictionaries, and to find an astronomical feature named after one of his works? *Random* and *Heritage,* among others, list Bradbury in this fashion; and a crater on the moon, *Dandelion,* has been named after one of his stories. The agents of these honors were lexicographers and astronauts; they were joined in the exercise of celebrating his talents, by his fellows, when the Writers Guild in 1974 presented him with its highest award.

However, it is not formal accolade or recognition that blazons Bradbury so much as the testimony of his many buffs. They come in all ages, and are scattered around the globe. Apparently he speaks with special felicity and clarity to the young. I know this from my own son, who at 15 could not have been less interested in my product or literary friends, until I once mentioned that I knew Ray Bradbury. Suddenly I became an interesting person.

Bradbury has the gift of enchanting the disenchanted. He has an ebullience that is all too rare in this plodding world. While his vision seems at times periscopically cosmic, he is always perfectly aware of what is going on at ground zero. He has been and continues to be outspoken on social issues— sometimes at 90- and 180-degree variance with my own views and perhaps some of yours, but what of that? He was a brave and vocal critic of the Vietnam madness long before the anti's became the majority. His creative thinking on city planning, rapid transit, the population explosion, the environment, the probing of space, make up a formidable body of opinion.

Also formidable, incidentally, are his titles. His very first book of stories, *Dark Carnival*, published when he was 27, has tight little one- and two-word names like *Skeleton, Reunion, Interim, Cistern, The Jar, The Lake, The Wind*; but as Bradbury's range expanded, so did his titles. They now go rolling on, mini-poems in themselves:

> *Boys! Raise Giant Mushrooms in Your Cellars!*
> *Dark They Were, and Golden-Eyed*
> *A Train Station Sign Viewed from an Ancient Locomotive Passing Through Long After Midnight*
> *Any Friend of Nicholas Nickleby's Is a Friend of Mine*
> *Emily Dickinson, Where Are You? Herman Melville Called Your Name Last Night in His Sleep*

The record for Bradbury to date is a title for which we make room above and below, so that it may be seen in all its splendid girth:

> *Mrs. Harriet Hadden Atwood, Who Played The Piano For Thomas A. Edison For The World's First Phonograph Record, Is Dead at 105.*

A few of Bradbury's early critics complained that he was humorless, like Whitman and Masters, but they have been silenced many times over. Some of the most delightful humor ever committed to paper circulates in such stories as *The Wonderful Ice Cream Suit* (Chicano), *Dandelion Wine* (midwest American) and *The Terrible Conflagration Up At The Place* (Irish). Bradbury's humor is warm, kindly and quiet; he leaves jokes and punning and slapstick to stand-up comics and pratfallers; he rarely goes to the spice shelf for satire or irony.

But there is a side of Bradbury's work less well known than it ought to be, and that is his poetry—his declared poetry, as against the generally poetic texture that is in his prose. Of his 15 books, only one is a collection of poems, and it goes by a title affectionately adjusted from Whitman: *When Elephants Last in the Dooryard Bloomed.* The 51 poems in the volume are wildly various, but most of them are made of the special sorcery that Bradbury practices. There are personal poems among them of such delicious flavor that you want to commit them to memory. One of my favorites, which can model for Daughter Mad." It will give you a fair idea of how sparkling the rest, is "The Boys Across the Street Are Driving My Young is the burgundy from Bradbury's vineyard:

> *The boys across the street are driving my young daughter*
>   *mad.*
> *The boys are only seventeen,*
> *My daughter one year less.*
> *And all that these boys do is jump up in the sky*
> *and*
> *beautifully*
> *finesse*
> *a basketball into a hoop;*
> *But take forever coming down,*
> *Their long legs brown and cleaving on the air*
> *As if it were a rare warm summer water,*
> *The boys across the street are maddening my daughter.*
> *And all they do is ride by on their shining bikes,*
> *Ashout with insults, trading lumps,*
> *Oblivious of the way they tread their pedals*
> *Churning time with long tan legs*
> *And easing upthrust seat with downthrust orchard rumps;*
> *Their faces neither glad nor sad, but calm;*
> *The boys across the street toss back their hair and*
> *Heedless*
> *Drive my daughter mad.*
> *They jog around the block and loosen up their knees.*

They wrestle like a summer breeze upon the lawn.
Oh, how I wish they would not wrestle sweating on the green
All groans
Until my daughter moans and goes to stand beneath her
    shower,
So her own cries are all she hears,
And feels but her own tears mixed with the water,
Thus it has been all summer with these boys
    and my mad daughter.

Great God, what must I do?
Steal their fine bikes, deflate their basketballs?
Their tennis shoes, their skin-tight swimming togs,
Their svelte gymnasium suits sink deep in bogs?
Then, wall up all our windows?
To what use?
The boys would still laugh wild a-wrestle
On that lawn.
Our shower would run all night into the dawn.
How can I raise my daughter as a Saint,
When some small part of me grows faint
Remembering a girl long years ago who by the hour
Jumped rope
Jumped rope
Jumped rope
And sent me weeping to the shower.

As a father, as a poet, as a holder of a distinguished seat in
the parliament of man, and as a proven friend of outer space,
Bradbury is exactly the right ambassador to be sent on the first
staffed rocket to Mars. He speaks fluent Martian, knows the
layout as nobody else, and, if any trouble should arise, he
could charm the antennae off the most restless native.

OPTIONS ON A
GOOD BOOK

THE BIBLE IS MORE THAN A FONT OF MORAL,
artistic, literary and religious inspiration. It is also a syllabus
of history and archeology whose validity keeps getting checked
out by discoveries such as the Dead Sea Scrolls, and by scientific findings. It is a working mine of ethics, too: a trove of
early philosophy and sociology and jurisprudence. And, although the authors of the Scriptures didn't bargain for it, it is
also a source of plays and movies.

This last gives rise to a question. Why, since the Bible is a
perennial best-seller, are so relatively few dramatizations based
on it? Down through the history of theater, the number of
plays written on biblical themes or characters would not ex-
ceed the hands slapped by the starting lineups of two college
basketball teams. From both Testaments, only Cain, Samson,
Saul, David, Jeremiah, Job, Jesus and Lazarus have been
worked importantly into plays. There have of course been

many productions of *The Passsion Play,* the most famous being the one in Oberammergau, but other versions have spread
well beyond the mountains of Bavaria to towns in Italy, Swit-
zerland and New Jersey, and westward to the Pilgrimage Bowl
in the highlands of Hollywood. These, however, must be
counted as essentially one play, with variations. All in all,
theatrical excursions into biblical territory still leave a million
square miles unexplored.

The movies have made a few passes, most of which turned
out to be grandiloquent kitsch: *Ben Hur, The Robe, King of
Kings, The Greatest Story Ever Told, The Ten Command-
ments, David and Bathsheba, The Story of Ruth, The Pass-
over Plot* and an anthological film with the smugly pompous
title, considering its claim, of *The Bible.* It took an Italian film
by Pasolini, austerely named *The Gospel According to St.
Matthew,* to breathe some kind of conviction into the character
of Jesus.

There are many reasons for the frequent lameness of biblical
pictures. Fear of offending parochialists and watchdogs of
dogma has to be a major block; so does uncertainty of approach to the language and idiom of biblical times, and the
difficulty of relating historic matter to the psychological con-
figurations of our day. Most of the famous scriptural characters
perform like wax figures animated by machinery: they speak
and act as though they were trained in Sunday schools and
seminaries rather than in drama courses.

The poetry and literary power of the original texts are almost never honored. In producing *The Bible,* Dino De
Laurentiis, who also made *King Kong,* could hardly have been
expected to exercise scruples about language. Writers of
biblical screenplays betray an understandable anxiety to avoid
the archaic, to be dignified without being stiff, colloquial with-

§ § § § § § § § § § § §

out being vulgar, and credibly human while still preserving an ambience of spirituality. Matters on which the 40 or so anonymous authors of the Bible wrote with wisdom and intuition have in our time been transmuted into disciplines and sciences, but most modern writers hesitate to apply insights informed by the likes of Freud and Jung because they are leery of trespassing on grounds of tradition.

"It is not enough," wrote the film critic James Powers, "simply to dramatize a biblical story, depending for significance on an original line from the King James version thrown in here or there, spoken resonantly, with a halo spot on the speaker." Nor can figures who loom large in canonical settings be represented as speaking like Merv Griffin or Gerald Ford. The thoughts of the eminences of Scripture were as a rule lofty, and their utterance passionate. But while we accept eloquence from all characters in Shakespeare except grave-diggers and menials (and even they are often witty and wise), we are somehow uneasy about the scripted eloquence of actors portraying prophets, psalmists, singers and kings of holy writ. And that, I think, is because Shakespeare comes to us whole and undiluted, in steadily pulsing iambic pentameter, whereas biblical drama must be superimposed on texts that were originally poems, essays, stories and parables. Shakespeare followed the sacred writings by anywhere from 1,500 to several thousand years: hence, from our point in time and language, he is that much more removed from deep antiquity and archaism. Moreover, Shakespeare wrote in our own, our native tongue, and did not have to be translated from the Hebrew, Aramaic and Greek.

But there are other considerations. The great lumpen bourgeoisie of letters, including many a critic, is hostile to heightened language. This partly explains the rarity of poetic drama in America's performing arts. So unaccustomed have we become to *attempts* at felicity and style in the language of theater and film, that most of us don't even know what to make of one when it comes along. A single biblical film, *The Story of Ruth,* drew from eight major reviewers in as many key cities around the country, the following contradictory estimates: "tasteless"; "told with taste and dignity"; "a muddled story"; "a beautiful story, beautifully told"; "horse opera dressed for ancient history"; "admirable for integrity and imagination"; "flat and cold"; "moving and tender."

There is no dearth of modest-budget short biblical films made by church groups and religious organizations for exhibition in social halls and sanctuaries, and these can afford to deal with lesser themes and subordinate people out of the Good Book. But major filmmakers are distinterested in any but the top biblical names. The star system applies to Scriptures no less than to Westerns. Jesus and Moses are of first rank—everybody has heard of *them.* David is of lower standing, but still strong enough to justify casting Gregory Peck in the role, as was done by 20th Century Fox in 1952. And it must be considered an extraordinary freak, a sport in the history of picture making, for the same studio to have produced, a few years later, a film about Ruth of Moab, starring an unknown Israeli actress.

There are a hundred fine biblical stories yet to be shot on film or tape, but entrepreneurs tend to be shy. If one adds to the Bible the largely magnificent Apocrypha, then the options and opportunities expand still further. Artists and composers long ago saw the possibilities in the dramas of Judith and Holofernes, Susannah and the elders, and the struggles of the Maccabees, but to my knowledge no movie has yet been undertaken on any of those themes. (James Bridie, Scotch playwright, wrote a thoroughly charming one-act play, *Tobias and the Angel,* based on the Apocryphal *Book of Tobit,* but try and find it performed anywhere.) The biblical *Book of Esther* has marvelous color, a strong story line, suspense, intrigue, vivid characters, great moral force, a confrontation with the idea of genocide which speaks to our day, and a catharsis that would send audiences home happy. I have long felt it would make a glamorous movie. But once, when I was working at Columbia Pictures as a producer, I wrote a memo to the head of the studio, Harry Cohn, suggesting that he consider making a film of *Esther.* Cohn was in Las Vegas for the weekend, and my suggestion went to him in a courier's pouch, along with other studio mail. When he received it, he was so impressed by my idea that he could not wait until he returned to Hollywood on Monday. He fired me before he went down to dinner.

For years a Hollywood studio fretted with an ambition to make a film out of Thomas Mann's monumental tetralogy, *Joseph and His Brothers.* Several screenplays were written, but the brew was too heady. The story, in the jargon of the trade, could not be licked. But then television arrived at the notion that a story need not be compressed into two, three or four hours. *Roots* went on for a week. And shortly afterward, along came Franco Zeffirelli with a six-hour dramatization of *Jesus of Nazareth.* It was no longer necessary to squeeze Joseph and his 11 brothers and the Ishmaelites and Potiphar and Mrs. Potiphar into a mere 90 minutes, less 18 for commercials.

After all, the events of our Revolutionary past were admitted to prime time in a flush of bicentennial specials, and it was discovered that audiences liked what they saw, and that this eruption of historical drama did no damage to the landscape: that instead it fertilized and improved it. Perhaps the same time and facilities will be afforded, one day, to the people and events of a still older and greater epoch in the history of our kind. The Bible can wait indefinitely for this to happen: the question is, can we?

TAKING CREDIT

CREDIT HAS BECOME A FORMIDABLE MULTIPUR-
pose word in our language, what with terrorists taking "credit"
for ghastly atrocities, millions of credit cards pulsing in the arteries of commerce, and all the media deeply involved with
credits in the sense of proper recognition for artistic and technical achievement.

There are up to 22 distinct meanings of credit in the bigger,
unhurried dictionaries, and most of the emanations are posi-
tive. Terms like *reliance, trust, truth, belief, faith, esteem,
commendation, good name, source of honor,* hover over credit
like bees around clover. It is only when we come to politics,
economics and show business that the definitions harden.

Whatever source of honor lies in machine-gunning inno-
cents at an airport, or murdering ambushed schoolchildren, it
is remote from the understanding of all except maniacal fa-
natics. As for the commercial aspect of credit, nobody has im-

proved on the formulation left us by the English philosopher John Locke 300 years ago: "Credit is nothing but the expectation of money, within some limited time."

But it is in the territories of authorship and attribution that credit has it most fascinating adventures. Plagiarism is of course the most morbid and perverted form of credit-taking. In a way it is brasher than outright stealing, since a common thief does not publicly display what he has stolen or claim it as his own in print. But the plagiarist has no such scruples. I once wrote an article titled *Mind You, I Love Radio* for a national magazine named *Stage,* published in New York. Not long afterward, in the *Montreal Herald,* a man named Glanzer, who described himself as a free-lance magazine writer, freely helped himself to my article. He changed the title to *I Actually Love Radio,* as though that would cover his traces, and proceeded to copy out the rest intact, except for a few inane localisms inserted as parentheses. The style and language of the original piece were such as to make it easily detectable, which is to say that it could in no way be confused with a weather report. My opening went:

"Mind you, I love radio. I love it because it squats in the sky and is bigger than the seven seas, yet it quivers like the needle of a compass and is faster than a wink. I love it because the turn of a bored engineer's wrist on 52nd Street can stir the heavens over China, and an actor saying that men from Mars are landing in New Jersey can send panic charging like a herd of buffalo across a continent."

Glanzer copied this word for word, except that he substituted "Montreal" for "52nd Street," and went on, sentence after sentence, paragraph after paragraph, lifting my text verbatim and passing it off as his own. Unadmirable as this piracy was, it ranked only a few degrees lower than my lack of response. I did nothing about it—a dereliction of my unwritten duty to other writers, and perhaps to society, considering that it should be the obligation of everyone to make theft as unrewarding as possible, short of joining the police. But at the time I was up against heavy work deadlines and other concerns; besides, I felt something like pity for this Quebecois *ganef,* who I figured must be either very young or senile, and maybe even hungry. Perhaps nothing justified inaction on my part; but lately I find that I am not the only writer who let a decade or two pass before recalling an atrocity of credit-snatching.

Helen Deutsch, a dramatist of many fine credits, including the films *Lili, The Seventh Cross* and *King Solomon's Mines,* contributed to the *Writers Guild Newsletter* an account castigating the late Paul Gallico for having taken a series of deep bows for work that was not his but hers. The explanation of what happened is as complicated as a tax form, but it boils down to the claim that the source for *Lili,* for whose screenplay Deutsch received an Academy Award nomination and Guild award, had been wrongly attributed to a short story by Gallico published two years *after* the film went into production. According to Deutsch, Gallico was not above "accepting awards and delivering lectures, etc., regarding his contribution to *Lili.* He had nothing whatever to do with it." When at the Cannes Festival the picture was given the Best Entertainment Award, "Gallico graciously arose and accepted the award for 'his film.' "

So-called fronting is another variety of credit manipulation. *The Front,* a picture of the obnoxious blacklist days in the first (and be it hoped, the last) McCarren-McCarthiad, is based on actual credit-finagling stratagems within the media. The story deals with a mousy restaurant cashier (Woody Allen) who, by arrangement, takes credit for a film written by a proscribed writer. This was common practice in the *Red Channels* era. It was the only way a blacklistee could make a living.

The infrastructure of credit determination and arbitration in the theatrical arts is long, wide, deep and labyrinthine, especially when it comes to writing. The credit provisions of the Writers Guild of America run to 28 single-spaced type-written pages packed with 60 separate articles and 51 a-b-c-d sub-articles. To the lay reader they are dizzying, but to the professional writer they represent years of struggle against moral and legal injustices in which credit was denied or mis-appropriated. Like all codifications, including the Ten Com-mandments and traffic ordinances, this index of credit pro-visions stands on a bedrock of experiences that were often bitter and ugly.

Even a hasty glance at the advertisements in the entertain-ment section of any newspaper will disclose at once a jungle of credits known in the trade as billing, whereby principal contributors to given works are listed. The relative positions of names spread out in any ad are never casually arrived at; at best, they are the fruit of negotiation; at worst, they are the issue of pitched battle which at times ends up in arbitration or a lawsuit. Order of listing, size of type, precedence or subse-quence to the title, differences between "starring," "co-star-ring," "featuring," even the placement of "and" and "with," or the setting-off of a name by framing a box around it as though to avoid contamination by other names, all these are ramifications of billing.

Elaborate machinery now exists for settling credit disputes, but in the archives of the creative arts unjustified credit has sometimes been given or taken innocently, as when original sources are lost in time, or records are vague. Did Beethoven write the *Jena* Symphony? Some think it was Michael Haydn. Did Shakespeare write the plays, or was it Bacon? Was it Purcell or Clarke who composed that disputed trumpet voluntary? Did David write the Psalms? If Franz Joseph Haydn didn't compose the *feldpartita* on which Brahms based his *Variations on a Theme by Haydn,* then who did? And why are certain things stubbornly attributed to the Glanzers of this world, when historians solemnly assure us the attributions are in error? They tell us Napoleon did *not* say, "England is a nation of shopkeepers"—a man named Paoli did. Personally I have never believed Plutarch's story that Diogenes, when asked solicitously by Alexander the Great if he (Alexander) could do him any favor, replied, "Yes, would you stand out of my sun a little." Maverick though he was, Diogenes would have had no reason to be rude to an emperor who approached him respectfully. I suspect that credit for the line belongs to some wag in Athens, perhaps a drinking companion who made up the story and told it to Plutarch over a bottle of wine in a tavern. In a modern and lesser context, one has only to think of the countless Goldwynisms attributed to Samuel Goldwyn. About one out of every 10 malapropisms credited to him actually were said by Goldwyn.

Two great names stand as pillars of mystery: Anon and Attrib. Most of the Bible, and the entire art and architecture of ancient Egypt, to mention only two massive entities, are from the hand of Anon. There should be a monument raised to him, just as there is for the Unknown Soldier.

It is sobering to realize that credit disputes reach even unto the highest places. They not only approach but go right past the throne of God. After all, credit for the creation of the world is given to God on the authority of Genesis 1 and 2; but some scientists and all atheists disagree. The trouble with attempting to determine *this* credit is that there is no known way to arbitrate it. And even if there were, there would be no way of appealing the judgment to a higher court.

BROUN

A NEW BOOK ABOUT HEYWOOD BROUN, JOUR-
nalist, has come out. It is the fourth I know of since he died
39 years ago, and I am by now encouraged to hope that his
memory will be with us indefinitely. For he was a boyhood
hero, and there were not many of those.

A hero is not necessarily a celebrity. I can think of no better
measure of the difference than one proposed by Daniel
Boorstin when he wrote, "The hero is distinguished by
achievement, the celebrity by his image; the hero creates himself, the celebrity is created by the media; the hero is a big
man, the celebrity is a big name."

Broun was big in every sense: He stood nearly six feet
four, and was—how shall I say it—fat. He shambled as he
walked, and wore disreputably scuffed and misshapen shoes.
Perhaps because his feet were so far from his head, he tended
to be absentminded about them. He once showed up at the

ultra-posh Park Avenue Racquet and Tennis Club wearing one black and one white shoe. People who did not love him called him a slob, but even Broun's friends acknowledged that he was a leading contender for the title of world's worst-dressed man.

One night after a Broadway opening, he ran into the play's producer in the lobby of the theater. The producer took a look at Broun's suit, which was rumpled as usual, and said, "That's a hell of a way to dress for my opening. Your suit looks as though you've slept in it."

"Now that you mention it," Broun replied, "I just woke up."

I first became a Broun fan at 17, when I got a job as a reporter on the *Greenfield Recorder*, a small-town daily in western Massachusetts. On the exchange desk every morning I found a collection of out-of-town newspapers including the *New York World,* for which Broun wrote a column. I read him religiously. Even to my boy's mind, Broun's humor, his lucidity, his compassionate liberalism, his empathy with the underdog and total absence of awe for the overdog, was deeply appealing.

One morning I wrote a letter to Broun. An entry in a vapid diary I kept refers to my having done so, but what I wrote— whether concerning one of his columns, or the state of the nation, or my own ambitions, or my admiration of him— whether it was a long or a short letter, I have no recollection. In any case, a week later I received a telegram from him, inviting me to see him when in New York. I was flattered by the implication of cosmopolitanism in the phrase "when in New York"; it was as though I had got a cable reading "when next on safari in Kenya." I had never been south of Coventry, R.I. Now that I had an invitation to call on my hero, I made it my business to get to the city. I wrote Broun that I would be down Saturday the 28th.

I was briefed by worldly colleagues on the *Recorder* as to how one got from Grand Central Station to Times Square. More helpful still was the use of the *Recorder*'s due-bill on the Hotel St. James in the West 40s.

I checked in at the St. James, and before I took my coat off, I telephoned Broun. To my chagrin there was no answer. Had my god of journalism and the humanities, the most important person with whom I had ever communicated, simply ignored my letter and forgotten his own invitation? Had he left the city for the weekend, not realizing that I was a working man, really a child laborer, who must be back at his $25-a-week job on Monday morning, Broun or no Broun? Had he gone out of the country, as a celebrity might easily do on an instant's notice, on a mere whim, especially here in New York where transoceanic ships were always departing and arriving? I was shaken by the no-answer, and tried again and again.

I distracted myself that evening by going to the Roxy theater. It had not been standing long, and was more splendid than Mr. Khan's pleasure dome in Xanadu; there was not the slightest intimation of mortality for either Mr. Rothafel, who had given the theater its cozy household name, or for the movie palace itself, whose life tenure, it turned out, was to be little more than that of the average horse. The show, whatever it was, enthralled me in short takes, due to the fact that I left my seat at intervals to try Broun's number.

I slept fitfully that night, my mission in jeopardy. How could I go back to Greenfield and tell my associates that I couldn't even raise Broun on the telephone? That all I had accomplished in New York City, seat of culture in the New World, was to go to a show at the Roxy, like any boob of a tourist?

In the morning I had the good sense to allow that Broun

might, if he were not in Paris or Casablanca, be sleeping late at home on a Sunday, and so I did not try his number until noon. There were several rings, and then—Eureka!—a man's voice. The party was foggy as to who Corwin of the *Greenfield Recorder* might be, until I reminded him of the telegram; then it came to him, and he apologized for the lapse and told me to come right up.

He lived at 333 West 85th Street, in an old brownstone. I was received in a room walled entirely by bookshelves from floor to ceiling, with every inch of space on the shelves occupied. Broun wore pajamas and a robe that hung on his huge bulk like a tired tarpaulin. His gunboat feet overflowed bedroom slippers that must have been too small to begin with, and the beginning lost in time. He asked many questions about myself, asked to see a sample of my work if I happened to have one with me, and it just so happened I had one with me. He scanned the column quickly and handed it back with a noncommittal smile, and told me to keep on writing, and not to be impatient with myself or the world.

Just before I left, he stood silent for a moment, as though trying to remember where he had put something, then he went out of the room and came back with a chair on which he stood to reach the highest of the bookshelves. He searched for a particular item, found it, got down off the groaning chair, and handed me a slim volume. It was a poetic fantasy entitled *Gandle Follows His Nose.*

"This," he said to me, "is the best thing I have ever written. I have only one copy left beside this one, and I want you to have it." He inscribed the book, pressed it in my hand, wished me luck, and walked with me to the door with his arm around my shoulder. I never saw him again.

Gandle Follows His Nose is short—189 mini-sized pages.

Broun probably followed his own nose when he wrote it, but
if he did, that was not a bad method, since he had a good
journalist's spontaneousness and polymer chains of poetic
ideas. The work has an improvised feeling, as though its author sat down to write it with only the vaguest idea, at first, of
who Bunny Gandle was and where he was going. But Gandle
turned out to be Everyman, especially a man named Broun.
And where Broun took Gandle was from birth to death, en-
countering on the way various people, dragons, sorcerers, an
affable genie and a two-headed god whose eyes were red currants and whose name was unmentionable.

It is a robust story, sentimental, allegorical, philosophical,
crowded with symbols and sequined with Broun's irrepressible
charm and humor. Yet Broun himself felt it held "a tragic
significance." Perhaps he meant the tragedy of existence,
which is certain of only one thing—its end.

Five years after my pilgrimage to Broun, he wrote a column
commenting on a rumor that he had died:

"After learning of the rumor I made a brief review of my
past and my prospects. I decided that I'd like a postponement
for maybe five years—maybe ten. I'd like to take one more try
at a novel. Once I wrote a book that pleased me to the hilt.
Few read it, and I seemed to be almost the only one who found
in it wisdom and a tragic significance. Once a year I read
Gandle and say to myself, 'You were good when you wrote
that.' Though I don't think I can better this book, which has
long been out of print, I'll take, I hope, at least one more jab
at the job. And after that, Mr. Gridley, you many fire when
you are ready!"

It was nine years before Gridley fired, but Broun never took
that one more jab at a novel. He was busy with other things,
like founding the American Newspaper Guild, a trade union,

against fierce and powerful hostility. Like the hero of his novel, Broun fought dragons and did his best to destroy unmentionable gods whose eyes were made not of red currants, but of current events. The passion and eloquence of his struggle to save Sacco and Vanzetti from official murder at the hands of a notoriously biased judge and a sanctimonious hand-washing governor's commission, was only one (albeit the best known) of Broun's many headlong chivalric forays against gargantuan windmills. Again and again he rode into battle like Quixote, except that his enemies were never chimerical or his motives antic. He strained, as few men of media have ever done consistently, for those elusive goals of truth and justice.

It is good that Broun's memory is regularly renewed and nourished by relays of biographers. Nobody writes much about his detractors, most of whom are forgotten, except the most vicious among them, Westbrook Pegler, the same who once condoned a lynching. Peg was a wise guy, an unremitting curmudgeon with an arresting turn of phrase, basically a pygmy in an accommodating jungle. Broun, on the other hand, was more like a colossus in the coliseum. May he rest in the peaceful satisfaction that it is getting along toward a half-century since he shambled and wrote among us, and he is still loved.

AVAST, YE GROANERS!

ONE OF THESE DAYS SOME BRIGHT DOCTORAL
candidate will come along and write a thesis on the low repute
of the pun in all the performing media. It is an odd phenomenon. The plenary groan that meets any pun ventured in
a lecture, on the stage, or in a TV talk show, is as automatic as
it is undiscriminating.

Now and then some brave nonconformist in an audience
will laugh at or even applaud a good pun, but mostly there is
a reflexive communal plaint, as though at an affront to public
morals. The irony is that such protest, although usually good-
natured, implies informed criteria, elevated taste or even
superior word skill on the part of the groaner, whereas as often
as not the deprecator's own facility with words ranges from
ordinary to nil. Indeed groaners as a class have long been suspected of being just plain envious.

Edgar Allan Poe believed that "those most dislike puns who

are least able to utter them." From Poe to Oscar Levant is a flying jump, but the two agree on the point. Levant: "A pun is the lowest form of humor—when you don't think of it first."

Punning is an ancient sport. The Greeks are responsible for the stately term paronomasia, and the Hebrews of old indulged in it famously. Obviously the battle lines between pros and antis must have been drawn long ago. Good men have taken up arms on both sides, although the heaviest artillery belongs to the allies of the pun. I need go no further than to mention the generalissimo, Shakespeare.

Still, Charles Lamb, no mean wit, felt that a pun is "a pistol let off at the ear, not a feather to tickle the intellect." And our own Oliver Wendell Holmes equated punsters with "wanton boys that put coppers on railroad tracks. They amuse themselves, but this trick may upset a freight train of conversation for the sake of a battered witticism." I would argue that if any train of conversation can be disastrously derailed by a mere copper on a track, it does not speak well for the railroad.

Boswell thought better of the pun. "No innocent species of wit or pleasantry should be suppressed; a good pun may be admitted among the smaller excellences of lively conversation." But Victor Hugo struck a classic balance: "Far be it from me to insult the pun. I honor it in proportion to its merits—no more." Which also implies no less.

All this brings me to Edwin Newman, broadcaster, whose book on the state of our language, *Strictly Speaking*, became a best-seller. The opening of his last chapter places Newman right alongside E. A. Poe in a forward trench: "There are millions of people who groan when they hear a pun. It is a standard response, and my impression is that they are simply envious or bent on denying themselves one of the delights that language offers."

Well and good; but then Newman declares, as though confessing, that he has openly punned for a long time, and claims "a small, if anonymous place in history" for one of his inventions. It seems that in 1945 he called a speech by James Byrnes "the Second Vandenberg Concerto" because of its similarity to a speech made by Senator Vandenberg a short time before. Newman goes on to explain that the phrase (a play on Bach's *Brandenburg Concertos*) was reproduced in Ambassador Charles Bohlen's *Witness to History*, "without," Newman pouts, "credit to me."

Still combing his adventuresome past, Newman then scolds *Time* magazine for using another of his puns, "Pompidou and Circumstance"—again without credit. That was careless of Bohlen and *Time*; but strictly speaking, *Strictly Speaking*, while delightful and salutary as a whole, falls down in its chapter on the pun. To begin with, puns on names are too easy. On Hugo's scale, they should not be honored more than they merit—and that is little. A name is fixed and has no elasticity.

One could just as easily say that critics tried to harry Truman; that the art dealer who bought *Arceaux Fleurs* got his Monet's worth; that Frankie singing under a full moon was a Moonlit Sinatra.

I myself have written name puns, but I make no historic claims for them. I proposed an epitaph for my friend Oscar Dystel, once editor of *Coronet*: "Lay that Dystel Down." And for the tomb of the Austrian composer Czerny (pronounced CHERnee) I offered "Czerny's End." Ambassador Bohlen can have them both.

There are ample grounds for grave humor, the most evident being the cemetery. An epitaph for one Mr. Box runs, "Here lies one box within another"; and there is a wry comment over the remains of an attorney named Strange: "Here is an honest lawyer, That is Strange." And so on and on. But the connoisseur of puns prefers a certain elegance, as in Sydney Smith, English clergyman of the nineteenth century, who said about two women who lived on opposites sides of the street and had loud disputes as they leaned out of their windows, that they could never come to any agreement because they were arguing from different premises.

There is today only one safe medium for the pun, and that is print. The same reader who groans at a pun on the stage or in a TV studio, where his reaction can be duly registered, relaxes and enjoys wordplay on the page. Only a Scrooge would carp on reading, atop an article about cannibalism in *Natural History,* the caption. "One Man's Meat is Another's Person." Or when Linus, in the comic strip *Peanuts,* threatens to sue the dog Snoopy for not returning his security blanket, and warns, "flea-bargaining won't help you, either!"

Sometimes the pun appears in a serious context. The *Southern Sierran,* deploring open-pit mining operations in Death Valley National Monument, ran an article entitled "Your Land—And Mined."

Travel and Leisure, in an article on music in Vienna, offered "Strauss in the Wind"; and *Westways* did even better with "Henry Miller at Eighty—Of Sound Mind and Bawdy." Paul Wallach, gourmet for all seasons and seasonings, described a seafood restaurant as being located near a "gull-meets-buoy seascape."

Contrived puns, like name puns, fly economy class. The more elaborate the setup, the lower the rating. Example: The South American liberator Simon Bolivar used to climb a watchtower at noon every day to watch pretty secretaries go by on their way to lunch. This got to be known as Bolivar

Watch Time. Then there was the greeting card picturing a golf course with Santa pitching a ball onto a pear-shaped green where a partridge is roosting. The legend: "And a partridge on a par three." It neglected to mention a birdie.

No news story is too small to invite a pun. An AP dispatch about a farmer who was wounded when his setter stepped on the trigger of his shotgun, carried the heading, "Master Is Wounded by Dog's Faux Paw."

Dogs seem to inspire puns. Some years ago I contributed one in the course of a broadcast. A certain dog who was listed in the files as an Auto Chaser and Tire Nipper Class 4, and known to the authorities as a mischief-making cur, was finally done in by a whitewall. As a result he was denied admission to Dog Heaven, and sent instead to Curgatory.

Happily, although the pun has been screened from the screen, barred from bars and held to be more odious than melodious on radio and TV, it has a haven and a protector. Perhaps the greatest citadel of the pun is the *Los Angeles Times*. It has the highest incidence and best punning average of any major organ in the world. Over a period of only a few weeks I logged among many others the following:

Sports page: A wrestling bear named Victor is undefeated in 10,000 matches against volunteers from our species. Headline: "Victor is Almost Unbearable."

Foreign news: Sophia, new Queen of Spain, enrolls in a humanities course at Madrid University. Headline: "Spain's Queen—A Touch of Class."

Jack Smith on plumbers in our society: "Plumbers Not All Drips."

Travel section: article on cremation rites in Indonesia: "No Crying In The Bier In Bali."

§ § § § § § § § § § § § §

Cecil Smith on the proliferation of auto-chase TV programs: "Things That Go Bumper."

Stan Delaplane on changes in the Colombian port of Cartagena: "City of Pirates on the Rum."

Bert Prelutsky on a Hollywood stunt man: "Best Feats Forward."

Baseball news: the California Angels acquire slugger Bobby Bonds: "More Security With Bonds."

Jack Smith on ugly buildings: "Edifice Wrecks."

Front page headline on expected volcanic eruption: "Mauna Loa Packs Hawaiian Punch."

Charles Champlin, on the ménage à trois in the film *Lucky Lady*: "The plot is unmenageable, trois as we will." This double-barreled pun brought two letters to the editor. One said, "Mais oui cinq Mr. Champlin for sharing his gifts with us." The other commented that "it was not bad for a triad a pun," but then cautioned that only God can make a three.

A crusty dissenter—a man with a lean and hungry look who *thinks* too much ("such men," as was said of Cassius, "are dangerous")—complained to me that the *L. A. Times* puns too much; that no serious journal should sanction paronomasia. Nonsense. Take the *New York Review of Books,* which is usually as solemn as a catafalque in the rain. An article by Robert Craft on sexploitation bore the title *Pay Dirt* and contained the confession, "I am not inspired by any lewd ambition at all, which, alas, could be a sign of Craft ebbing." *Esquire* ran an article on knives of quality, entitled *Blades of Class.*

Oddly enough, puns do not often appear at titles for plays or movies. Of 600 plays listed in Shipley's *Guide to Great Plays,* there is not a single pun. The only one I can think of is

not a very great play—Peter Ustinov's *Romanoff and Juliet.*
The National Film Board of Canada made a serious and important documentary on being overweight, and named it *A
Matter of Fat.* I can recall no other punned movie titles. On
the other hand, books and stories, being purely literary, abound
in them. A collection of Hyman Kaplan stories by Leo Rosten
is called *O Kaplan! My Kaplan!* A slim volume in which
fresh and irreverent captions are given to old masterpieces of
painting appears as *Captions Courageous.* A collection of
poems and prose by one of the former Beatles is entitled *John
Lennon In His Own Write.*

The interlingual pun is another species which has had happy
innings, especially in loose translations from the French. A book
called *Fractured French* includes the following: *C'est a
dire* (she's a honey); *Jeanne D'Arc* (no light in the bathroom);
coup de grâce (lawn mower)); *s'il vous plaît* (not sterling); *Ile
de France* (I'm sick of my friends); *entrechat* (let the cat in);
Marseillaise (mother says yes). As for German, Peter de Vries
wrote that *Gott Mit Uns* always sounded to him like a declaration that one had gloves.

Several correspondents, knowing of my addiction to puns,
have favored me with specimens. George Movshon, opera
critic, sent "a few thoughts occasioned by the recent appearance of a dramatic soprano who is almost literally five-by-five,
in the role of Aida. I was moved to suggest some suitable
operas for her future appearances: *Don Carload, Enorma,* the
title role in *The Masked Ball, La Fatso del Destino,* and of
course Verdi's *Fatstuff.*"

George Warren of Van Nuys wrote, "Watergate may have
produced little else of value, but it did give us a great pun,
attributed to Nixon staffer Leonard Garment, who observed
during the Battle of the Tapes, that 'Stonewalling doth not

misprision make.' " (That one is helped by the knowledge that misprision means misconduct, especially in office.) Mr. Warren also contributed one of his own puns about a musical based on the story of an 18th-century surgeon who made a name for himself by operating on the ailing thyroid gland of a famous German *dichter*. The title: *Getting Goethe's Goiter*. For readers under the age of 29, it should be explained that *Getting Gertie's Garter* was a hit musical of times past.

Walter Richards of Glendale wrote, "A pun, to be a classic, should have a nuance that appears upon a second hearing," and gave as an example, "Captious was a supercilious Roman Senator with a brother named Capricious." He then added, "the only problem with this one is that not enough people know the meaning of captious, so they miss the full implication of the pun." He must include me among the missers, because I didn't get it. Captious means disposed to find fault, and capricious means apt to change suddenly. Obviously I missed something. Now if a man lived on the island of Ischia, which is across from Capri, you might say that he would have been capricious if he were not ischiadic, which means sciatic, or suffering from sciatica, and you would have an unassailable pun. But it would hardly be worth the trouble.

A good example of the kind of pun Mr. Richards had in mind when he referred to the nuances, is a reported exchange between James Agate and Alan Dent:

Agate: Can ghosts be angry?

Dent: What else is there to do in the shades except take umbrage?

The brothers M. J. and J. M. Cohen, in their Penguin compendium of quotes, cite a notice posted in a New York corsetiere's: "We take you in so the boys will take you out."

It is perhaps to be expected of S. J. Perelman, one of the

grandest stylists in all humor, that his titles should pun with reckless abandon: *Stringing Up Father; Little Boy Grue; Methinks He Doth Protein Too Much; Pain Counterpane; Rancors Aweigh; Columbia, The Crumb of the Ocean; Whereas in Sulks My Julia Goes.*

There was a fine literary agent in Hollywood, a man of culture and a former writer, who for years signed every letter he sent out (there were thousands) with the complimentary close, "Ten per sentimentally." He was the late Dick Irving Hyland, and he was a brave fellow.

MIRACLES AND
§§§§§§§ DEMONS §§§§§§

PRAYER FOR THE 70s

We print your name on dollars
And are sure you stand over everything we say is under God
And all nations assume you are on their side and always have been,
*   war in and war out*
And every religion understands you better than every other reli-
*   gion, and you in turn lean toward each with special inclina-*
*   tions.*

You are called on to bless babies and aircraft carriers
And you are ceremoniously and endlessly praised on the basis that
*   flattery will get us somewhere.*

But there are those who pray as though tendering a bribe payable
*   on installments*
So as to accumulate years in this life and credits in the next
Some of us make you out a broker who supplieth needs and wants
Attorney who defendeth against hard claims

*Expunger of guilts who cleareth the conscience so we may be free
    to muck it up again*
Housekeeper of the soul who cometh in to clean once a week;
King of accountants auditing our secret selves,
*Liquidating our trespasses as we liquidate those who trespass
        against us,*
Keeping batteries of books filled with fateful identifications,
Entering as much the fall of a sparrow as the crash of a plane.

*We have heard it said you are not so smart after all, since it is
    unlikely you could add as fast as a computer or remember
    half so much*
*And although you are known to be more than generous in the
    number and variety of species, there seems to be little ra-
    tionale for the mosquito and less for plague bacilli.*

There have been complaints against you, charges of malfeasance,
*Implications of sleeping on the job, trigger temper, proneness to
    vengeance,*
*Tantrums of wrath that have consumed too many of the innocent
    with too few of the heinous.*

*Some of your public begrudge you the benefit of doubt and doubt
    your beneficence*
*Protesting that it was antic of you to have sponsored us to begin
    with, if we are to swarm like maggots on a rind too meager
    to support our duplicating billions.*

Some say the noblest ideas were set down by man
*And that you have been served by holy ghost writers beyond your
    deserts*
*They say that the whole conspicuous distance between the worm
    and Einstein, the drone of the bee and Beethoven,*
The entire interval, has been filled with struggles trailing blood:

§ § § § § § § § § § § § § §

Prayer for the 70s

Ages of frightened proto-men, heavy with ignorance, recoiling
    from fangs of fire, drowning in profligate floods, perishing
    in temblors, staggering into the unknown,
Their wails and brute chants and broken grunts fructifying at last
    into songs and sonnets and hallelujahs to your glory.
—Well, dissidents suggest that during this grand span you sat it
    out; that in the vasty meanwhile you went off to fish in
    deeper currents.

Lately it is announced that you are dead
Which means several things besides the receiver being off the
    hook when we dial you
It means that time must carry on by itself
And stars pinwheel through incandescent deserts and bottomless
    voids, all on an orderly hunch
It means the arching upward from the mud has been a drunken
    course, and purposeless, and hardly worth the trip
It means the very mansion of existence has no windows, and is
    just a big white elephant boarded up and haunted by your
    mistakes
It means that springtime is a come-on and a put-on, and not at all
    a show of dogged life, a riot of chlorophyll, a surge of sap and
    elixirs from wells so deep no radar pulse can ever return to
    tell what and where it touched
It means that the love of man and woman is a table of percentages,
    and their desire a disease of the id
It means that birth is a happening between pills
And old age a phase held together by plastic parts
It means the heart of man is replaceable as soon as the donor is
    legally dead
And death is a package deal with the best advertised mortuary.

So, God: if you are alive and in that heaven we have come to
    know is spotty with systems of gravity each pulling for itself

*Then perhaps you must flex the muscle of divine authority to get
　　　back in office*
*Because your antique miracles have been trumped by solemn
　　　science:*
*Daily the patent office registers intenser magic than the burning
　　　bush:*
The serpent from the rod becomes a ruby laser
The leper is healed by mycins
The blind draw vision from an eye bank.

*That being the case, dear busy God, please manifest thyself
　　　again through one superlative, new-minted covenant:*
*Create for the lot of us—all nations indivisible—an Act of God
　　　more stupendous than mere parting waters or a standing sun*
*A miracle harder to come by, that would, if consummated, cause
　　　dry bones from all the hundred holocausts to meet and dance*
*And charter stars to sing together in the brightest chancel of
　　　imponderable space*

And this is what that miracle would be:

That man should love his kind in all his skins and pigments,
And kill no more.

Repeat:
That we should love our kind
And kill no more.

Yes, granted, such a miracle is asking very much of you
But it is long past time to ask.

VISIT FROM A DEMON

I ASKED A DEMON TO LUNCH ONE DAY. I HAD
seen *The Exorcist,* and was curious to know whether the film
faithfully represented any particular class of fiends. The demon
did not come for lunch because he was fasting, but he did
appear, although not in the usual sense of that word, since he
was invisible like the antagonist in *The Exorcist.* That is where
the similarity ended.

I asked my visitor if he would object to being recorded on
tape. Not only did he not object, but he complimented me for
asking. "Already," he said, "you show a more rational approach than anything which appears in that film."

"In what way, pray?" I asked. Instantly, I realized this was
not the choicest expression to use with a demon, but he
brushed aside the slip. "Already you have taken the logical
step of wishing to record an encounter which would naturally
seem bizarre to whole communities of scientists, religionists

and thinking people. In the film, on the other hand, none of the adult principals sees fit to record any of the remarkable phenomena which occur every five minutes—phenomena such as throwing people out of windows; raising bodies horizontally without any visible means of support; levitating a heavy bed in the same fashion; causing a viscous green effluent which looks like rejected pea soup to be vomitted with great force in a priest's face; spewing a brownish substance which resembles infant do-do, and scoring a direct hit on a second priest's left eye; causing a little girl's head to turn a full 360 degrees, like the rotating beam of a lighthouse; making sounds like an angry menagerie at feeding time; cracking masonry as though by earthquake ('Must be rats in the attic,' says the girl's mother); raising welts on the child's bare abdomen, which spell out in cursive letters, 'Help me'; shouting loud obscenities in a coarse voice; arbitrarily stripping skin from the calf of the possessed child, leaving a wound too large to be covered by a Band-aid; murdering a movie director; attempting to assault an exorciser by crushing him with a massive wardrobe that moves around by itself; forming opaque white cataracts over both eyes of 12-year-old Linda Blair; cracking her lips; aging her skin and hair; giving her leprous lesions of the face and perhaps elsewhere; ventilating her bedroom with sudden gusts and squalls of cold air, when any demon in his right mind knows that warm air, not cold, is the preferred atmosphere. Need I go on?"

"No," I granted, "all that does happen in the film, and more. But what would you have had the adult principals do?"

"I excuse the child's mother because she is understandably hysterical, as well as somewhat of a pill. But Father Karras, a highly educated psychiatrist priest, and his colleague, the elderly archeologist Father Merrin (Max Von Sydow), might have advised the media of the unusual events going on in that house in Georgetown. If not the media, then scientists; if not scientists, then students of psychic phenomena; or, if the clerics wanted to keep the matter wholly within their church, they could have invited high-ranking observers from the Vatican—or, to satisfy the left wing of the church, Father Berrigan. Because for the two priests to keep the graphics of this sensational case to themselves, when even a fuzzy eight-millimeter home movie would supply a whole millenium of scholarly, scientific and religious inquiry, and perhaps help solve the 'mystery' of Good and Evil—for the two priests, I say, to keep all of that to themselves, was extremely shortsighted."

"But," I objected, "wasn't the important thing to relieve that poor girl of her distressing symptoms? To drive out the demon, rather than make the child a laboratory object?"

"Nothing would have driven out that demon faster (if it *was* a demon) than to have reporters from the *Washington Post* and the *New York Times,* the science editors of *Time* and *Newsweek,* Dr. Karl Menninger, Norman Vincent Peale, I. F. Stone, Walter Cronkite and a television crew in that bedroom. The demon would have gotten out so fast it would make your head spin like that little girl's, clear around."

" 'If it *was* a demon,' you say. Do you doubt it?"

"No respectable demon would choose to possess, at random, an innocent 12-year-old WASP child in the District of Columbia. What would be the point of it?"

"Then does the situation or importance of a victim count?"

"It helps. As we say, 'May the devil take the foremost.' "

"You mean a demon might prefer to possess a president?"

"One already has."

"Would you care to name him?"

"You have had 37 presidents. It's your guess."

"Let's get back to *The Exorcist*," I suggested, not wanting to discuss domestic politics with a visitor from a foreign principality. "I take it, then, that you hold a dim view of the demon in that film?"

"Correct. And the director of the film, himself, gives the audience a dim view of the demon late in the story. On camera, Satan, it turns out, is large, brooding, Caucasian, and has wings. Now that, sir, it total twaddle, since true demons are unphotographable. This movie demon is stupid, and vulgar beyond all conscience. He is also Iraqi, I believe. I did not read Mr. Blatty's book, but Mr. Von Sydow as the archeologist spends a whole long prologue poking among digs in Iraq. The good Father picks up a small stone demon's head and dusts it off. That apparently liberates this boob of a fiend, and the next thing you know, it has made its way across the world and up the Potomac to Washington, D.C. There are almost four billion people in this world, and millions of square miles of habitable land, and this demon has to pick out a nice little girl in an upstairs room of a house in Georgetown."

"Then you feel that the demon and the evil he perpetrates are superficial?"

"You can say that again. Demons are subtle, not brash. They insinuate, not insult. They assume a wide variety of forms and identities, allegorical and otherwise. For example, the serpent in the Garden, Adolf Hitler, Joe Stalin. I have never known a qualified demon to utter an obscenity. That would be altogether too common, since spoken obscenities may be heard on most stages and screens today (except on television screens, and that may come in time). The routine patois in the ranks of the armed forces is hardly hymnal, and the street talk of most central cities is rich in four-letter words and their deriva-

§ § § § § § § § § § § § §

tives. Also, when did you last read *Playboy, Penthouse, Hustler, Screw . . .*?"

"Tell me, is it true that the director of *The Exorcist* considers it 'a great, great story'? I thought I read that somewhere."

"Yes; the director, William Friedkin, has been quoted as saying that, above all, his picture is 'a great, great story concerning the mystery of goodness and the mystery of faith.' "

"The only mystery," observed the demon, "is how Mr. Friedkin could make such a silly, silly statement. Goodness and faith have nothing to do with the demonizing and un-demonizing of that girl. There is no question whatever of the girl's goodness or the demon's badness; and as for faith, the demon in the story has as much faith in his evil as the priests in their deity. What it comes down to is a test of stubbornness, not of faith. The picture degenerates into a loud, protracted tug-of-war between the powers of green-pea vomit and holy water, between words out of Scripture which were never intended for purgative rituals, and the obscenities of a screenplay."

There was a moment of silence. I broke it. "Mr. Friedkin has also been quoted as saying, 'There are only three reasons to make a movie—to make people laugh, to make them cry, or to frighten them.' "

"There is a fourth reason," replied the demon, and I thought I saw some dust rising from a shelf of books near where I assumed he was sitting. "To make people think."

"Oh, that," I said.

"Yes."

"Do you think perhaps there are not enough people who think enough about not thinking enough?"

"I think," said the demon, "that it is time to go." He sighed wearily, and that was the last I heard from him.

§ § § § § § § § §

MEDIA,
EQUIVOKES,
§ § § SNOBS, PIFFLE § § §

VERY NICE, VERY NICE

IGOR STRAVINSKY AT 25 WROTE HIS FIRST SYM-
phony. He was an aspiring nobody at the time, and the work,
which was as academic in form as a cap and gown, showed
little of the genius that made him, only five years later, one of
the most talked-of composers in the world. Reminiscing many
years afterward about that first performance of his Opus 1,
Stravinsky recalled that when it was over, Glazounov, then
43 and famous, came up to him and said, "Very nice, very
nice." Stravinsky took that as a bad omen, an obvious damna-
tion with faint praise.

The language of the gentle letdown is various, and has
been carefully developed over millenia. I have a hunch that
when Krong, a mural painter in prehistoric Altamira, finished
one of those fabulous bisons which ornament the roof of the
cave, a shaman of the tribe, after a long judicial squint and a
grunt or two, said, "Well, it's coming."

If such was the case, nothing much has changed. The odds are about 10 to one that if a playwright today invites a peer to a rehearsal of his new play, the inevitable critique will include the phrase, "It needs work." That is the safest of all possible judgments, since there has probably never been a rehearsal in the entire history of the performing arts which did not generate notes for some change, cut, emphasis or technical improvement.

The ambiguities and glosses of criticism (when personal, as in the case of Glazounov and Stravinsky) are meant to be kind. Glazounov, director of the Conservatory, creator of the highly successful *Raymonda* and *The Seasons* ballets, member of the musical hierarchy, was certainly not going to crush an eager young student by telling him that his work was derivative, uneven, and at times dull. But neither would he perjure himself by saying that the symphony was superb, inspiring or different. At such a moment, "very nice" is convenient; it comes as close to being unenthusiastically approving as one can be short of "okay" or "adequate." "Nice" in this context means nothing beyond passable, and the "very" gives it no support whatever—it is as innocuous as the very in "very sincerely yours."

Teachers and critics cannot afford ambiguity, but some intelligent people are constitutionally unable to offend or discourage by adversely criticizing the work of sensitive friends or acquaintances. And when these observers are also too honest to lie or mislead by unmerited praise, they tend to seek refuge in a form of double-talk, from which the artist may infer a compliment at his own risk. If one is not practiced in the art of the equivoke, he may need some suggestions, so I composed a few comments that could be construed as complimentary without committing yourself:

So few people put things together the way you do. (Thank God!)

I can't tell you all the thoughts it stirs up in me. (Not without losing you as a friend.)

I see where you are going. (Not very far.)

It has continuity. (So do aimlessly wandering ants.)

It certainly has your stamp on it. (Cancelled.)

It is beyond my expectations. (Worse than I thought it would be.)

It invites all sorts of striking comparisons. (Three strikes.)

It leaves me speechless. (One can fudge only so far.)

I can't begin to do this honor. (No way.)

Knowing of my interest in equivokes, William Ludwig, a screenwriter of distinction, sent me a set of seven which are applicable to movie productions—swivel-type critiques capable of being construed as compliments without at the same time perjuring the critic. Each was equipped by Mr. Ludwig with a parenthetical aside:

That artwork on the main titles—fabulous! (The picture went downhill from there.)

You couldn't have made this picture 10 years ago. (Audiences would have wrecked the theater. Now they take anything.)

You've plowed a lot of fresh ground here. (Fertilized it, too.)

Wowee! You sure have a piece of film there! (A pity it's been exposed.)

It's going to cause a lot of talk. (It may even cause you to lose some assignments.)

A new approach—that's what it is. (Imagine 10,000 feet of film and nothing worth looking at.)

I can understand why you were two years in production. (It

always takes longer when you don't know what you're doing.)

These are noble additions to the literature of the equivoke, division of cinema, and they entitle Mr. Ludwig to automatic membership in the American Society of Amphibologists, a nonprofit organization with headquarters in Dodge, Nebraska, known to *equivoquistas* as What a Place.

Now while the Society cannot supply funds for creative contributions of this nature, it is entirely proper to offer a matching set:

How on earth did you ever *conceive* it? (Stoned, probably.)

It has power. (The power to empty a theater in 10 minutes.)

I was riveted to my seat. (By the inability to get up and walk out without offending.)

You've *made* it! (And you'll have to live with it.)

It has class. (Fourth class.)

It will last. (Two days, and then be yanked.)

I haven't had a thrill like this in a long time. (Not since I accidentally picked up a live electric wire.)

All of the above are suitable for speaking or writing, if not for framing. But I am advised by Consuela de Cordoba of Forest Hills, L.I., that there is a species of *silent* equivokes, entirely gestural, which are even more noncommittal. By a simple sage nodding of the head, up and down, in the classical "yes" configuration, you will be interpreted as approving, whereas you would actually be saying to yourself, "Yes, yes, yes, this confirms what I have suspected right along—that Malcolm has no talent." Even the side-to-side movement, the standard *negative* headshake, will, if your eyes are closed and your expression rapt, be taken by Malcolm to mean that you find his film so marvelous you just can't put it into words. Other gestural equivokes are a pat on the shoulder or an embrace; both will be understood to mean, "You son of a gun, you *delivered!*" Actually the pat could mean, "I give you credit for having the courage to show the film"; the embrace could be a stroke of sympathy: "I commiserate with you in your time of trouble."

Naturally equivokes are more needed in one-to-one situations, where you are the sole audience, than when others are present, as at the screening of a film; in the latter case, you are partly insulated: your fellow sufferers take some of the pressure off you by making comments of their own. But if, say, you are visiting the studio of an artist friend, and he shows you an enormous wall-sized canvas painted entirely black except for a single green pea in the upper left corner, it is well to have a few equivokes ready. Here are some possibilities:

It's there. It's all there. (Seventy cans of Midnight Black.)

This could start a movement. (Toward the door.)

No one is going to take this lightly. (It must weigh a ton.)

It shows restraint. (You could have painted a *dozen* peas.)

It's clear and bold; nothing amorphous. (You could have painted mashed peas.)

Are you ever going to doubt yourself again? (It might help.)

It makes me think of Miro. (Jerry Miro, a house painter from Tenafly, N.J.)

The equivoke evades, certainly, but I still think it is a more worthy citizen of the arts than the savage clobbering not infrequently visited upon works judged to be inferior. One may enjoy the wit, compression, hyberbole or fireworks of slam reviews, but I, for one, feel for the victims the way I suppose a dissenting spectator in the Circus Maximus must have felt during the part of the entertainment where the martyrs were fed to the hungry lions.

There are performing critics who put on a show of their

own, and sometimes they are more entertaining than the subjects of their reviews. Only the playwright and his family could fail to be amused by Dorothy Parker's one-line dismissal of a Broadway production: *"The House Beautiful* is the play lousy." Or by Kenneth Tynan's 10-line review of a film in which the key sentence read, "The running time is 115 minutes; the walking-out time is much earlier." But I feel a little guilty at times, chuckling over this sort of shaft, because there is an overcast of sport at someone's expense. I am too aware of the tendency of all but the most serenely confident artists to believe everything bad that is printed about them. Cornelia Otis Skinner once said of opening night reviews, "It's as though some poor devil were to set out for a large dinner party with the knowledge that the following morning he would be hearing exactly what each of the other guests thought of him."

Detraction has its joys, and if you don't believe it, just make note, at your next dinner party, of the rapture with which somebody (there is always at least one) runs down a work or a person. W. H. Auden, himself a part-time critic, confessed that one cannot write a bad review without showing off. That may be an overstatement, but not by much.

Critics are my fellow practitioners oftener than they are my judges, and when they bring sound judgment and learning to their estimates, they can perform high and constructive services to both artist and audience. But I think it would do no harm for each of us to pin up on his bulletin board the sentiment of a rare gentleman of Massachusetts, one Emerson, who put it this way: "Criticism should not be querulous and wasting, all knife and root-puller, but guiding, instructive, inspiring, a south wind, not an east wind."

Nothing equivocal about that.

MORE FUN THAN FUN

WHY DO THE ARTS ATTRACT SO MANY SMITHS
and wrights and artificers to their domain? Is it because they
are a living? But so are mining and plumbing and selling. I
suspect it is because the arts invite the kind of work that seems,
or is to the initiate, a variant of play.

"Work is much more fun than fun," declared Noël Coward,
a licensed member of the theatrical calling. And while Coward
had no rank as a philosopher (there are some who dispute even
his standing as a playwright), he knew and worked with
enough fine artists to substantiate that judgment.

I can never hear the word *opera* or *opus* (the first began as
the plural of the second; only later did *opera* take on a special
musical meaning) without thinking of the universal phenomenon that is work. "A new work," we say, when something
respectable comes along. It may not stay respectable for long,
after the critics get through with it, but it is still called a

work. The term is its birthright, and should as well be its deathright.

"Work" has something of majesty in it, when applied to the end product of creative power. "An honest man is the noblest work of God," said Alexander Pope. Whereupon Robert Ingersoll turned it around to say that an honest god was the noblest work of man. There is certainly a divine aura about works of genius, and a perceptible glow around sheer monumentality. But the latter tends to be transient. "My name is Ozymandias, king of kings," wrote Shelley in the sonnet of the same name: "Look on my works, ye Mighty, and despair!" These works, Shelley gave us to understand, crumbled until nothing but empty beer cans and cigarette packs remained on the lone and level sands stretching to the nearest highway. On the other hand, when we look on the works of a Shakespeare, a Michelangelo, a Bach, despair is the last thing we feel; instead, we take fresh heart.

I think what makes the arts and their in-laws, the media, so compelling, is the *nature* of the work that goes into them. Yet in considering the concept of work as a life force, I found myself digressing, drifting afield of the context of media, and chasing after the idea that however vividly colored the spectrum bands of the working arts may be, they are only part of a very wide human range. When Hamlet mused, "What a piece of work is a man!", he tempted us to turn around in the contrary spirit of Ingersoll, and muse back to him, "What a piece of man is work!" Especially could this be said by any of us who is asked, as I have been, whether we would consider giving up work altogether. As much ask us if we should give up love. The two have much in common; between them they share dominion over our lives. Without enough of either we are in straits.

Work and love both have the power to fetter or to liberate, to injure or heal, to wither or fructify. Both can decay into baleful obligation; both can be sparkling or dull, fascinating or burdensome. Tokens of their association appear often. "Labor of love" is one. "Work," said Kahlil Gibran, "is love made visible." The common phrase to describe a bankrupt marriage is, "Married, but not working at it."

The dream of the prophets was for love to rule the earth. Actually it is work that rules the earth, and always has, since man first took on the habiliments of what, for better or worse, we call civilization. There is nothing that we wear, use, eat, nothing on our shelves, in our closets, files, vaults, nothing that we read or say or even *know*, that does not represent the work of people living and dead. All that we have learned has come to us through the work of workers immemorial; education is the filtration of billions of man-hours of study and creativity in the arts and sciences.

We communicate by words that were minted, wrought, jointed, conjugated, inflected by workers in language. The sublimest music, the highest reaches of philosophy, the brightest efflorescences of the human spirit, trace back to work, to galactic prodigies of work.

It is something to contemplate, standing in the circle of stones at Stonehenge, that at this moment we are in touch with bands of Neolithic men who hauled 45-ton sarsen blocks from God-knows-where, up a nine-degree gradient to this site. The sweat of those workers has hardly dried after 3200 years. Neither is it gone from the ruins of Baalbek, the Quetzalcoatl of Mexico, the great tomb of Osaka, the Ziggurat of Ur, the Chinese Wall.

The buttons on a shirt, no less than the pyramid of Cheops, symbolize labor. The faucet water that washes the dinner dishes had to be tapped, impounded, purified, pumped and piped. The pen in hand, the paper on the desk, the desk on the floor, the floor on the foundation—all are made, not grown. And the oldest work of all, of course, is agriculture. Endless sowing, plowing, reaping, threshing, harvesting. Man's needs have made working gardens out of steppe, upland, forest, terraced mountains and the weed-beds of the sea.

Next in scale to the mantle of the globe itself are the works that cover it; for Earth is an inutterably huge monument to work—to outpourings of thought and energy preserved in the forms of cities; to actualized architecture, frozen engineering, to the consolidated residua of the lifting and hauling and straining of myriads of workers, displayed in every last bridge, tunnel, dam, cathedral, skyscraper, depot, highway, vehicle—revealed in every line of print, every inch of fabric, every pane of glass, every ray of artificial light. Work is a force as inexorable as the tides.

When I am asked whether I would voluntarily give up work, I am set to stammering. Perhaps if I were a digger whose back had stiffened, a watchmaker whose eyes had dimmed, a ballplayer whose bones had become brittle, I would entertain the notion of calling it quits. Perhaps if I were ill, or fatigued, or bored, or if I were a millionaire not interested in acquiring another million, and I felt I could be happy idling in neutral, I would work no more. But I am a writer, and I like to think that I think at my job; and although it is never easy, I would no more voluntarily give up work than I would unwittingly give up thinking.

I suppose it fair to ask *why* we should want to go on working. Why *not* enjoy those palpable pleasures of sun, sea, the seasons, travel, sport, "entertainment"? But there is a kind of labor to pleasure, too. Many of us come home worn out from vacations. There is sometimes a grimness to the pursuit of a good time. The faces of people at bars, around gambling tables and in ear-crunching discotheques, are not exactly mirrors of joy.

Is it necessity that keeps us working? Neurosis? Expression? Compulsion? Fear of atrophying if we quit? Or is it the need to feel that we are useful, that we are pulling our weight, that we are of account. One cannot and should not rule out lesser inspirations. Gain, for example. It is not to be despised, except when it is the overwhelming first energizer—and not even then, if feeding the kids depends on it. The seeking of applause, too, is a motive, especially in the arts. Suppress it as we will, the child in us strains for approval.

Yet beyond these platforms, there is something mysterious, beckoning, and ineffable, that exerts a steady pull even on those who have more than enough money, and are sated with kudos. Work is to be done if for no other reason than the good one given for wanting to climb the highest of the mountains— because it is there. Call it Work Ethic, call it need to express, call it a way of keeping out of trouble, call it burden or obsession, blessing or curse; it is there. Small wonder it is mentioned oftener than love in that anthology of treatises on man and morality that we call The Bible.

THE IRON BED

PROCRUSTES WAS A BANDIT. IT IS WELL TO RE-
member that about him, before enlarging on his custom of
tying victims to an iron bed and then adjusting them to its
length by stretching those who were too short or amputating
those who were too long.

Theseus, second only to his cousin Hercules as the mightiest
of the classic do-it-yourself supermen, got rid of Procrustes
along with other nogoodniks on the road to Athens, but it was
the highwayman, and not the hero, whose example has sur-
vived to govern most of the media today.

The Procrustean principle has absolute authority in TV and
radio, where the clock is boss; it also rules, although not quite
so relentlessly, in newspapers and magazines, where space
becomes the iron bed; it is least felt in books and movies, which
is why so many novels and pictures go on too long.

Up to a point, it is a good thing to say what is to be said

succinctly and to avoid excess. Nobody complains about the arbitrary physical limits of the sonnet, the haiku, the short story, the musical overture. Indeed the discipline of meeting these limitations is part of the craft, and oftener than not, tonic to it. Conversely, no muralist argues that the spatial demands of filling a large wall or ceiling are too great; that the chapel should be cut down in size. But in the performing arts, length and space are inexorable forces, and here Procrustes gets into the act every day of the week, every minute of the hour.

Take TV news, for example. The average network news program has about 22 minutes to present nine or ten items, and the inescapable result of this is to compress, to synopsize, to oversimplify. For fuller details read the morning newspaper—providing the story will not be crowded out there as well, by other stories. A major radio news station has a slogan which it repeats throughout the day: "Give us 22 minutes, and we'll give you the world." No doubt the world has grown smaller—but *that* small?

Erik Barnouw, in his book on the evolution of American television, *Tube of Plenty*, recalls that in an early TV series entitled "Man Against Crime," a formula device was used for regulating length. Writers for the program (there were 50 different ones in the course of the series) included a "search scene" near the end of each program:

"The hero-investigator would search a room for a special clue. A signal would tell Ralph Bellamy how long to search. If time was short, he could go straight to the desk where the clue was hidden; if there was need to stall, he could first tour the room, look under old cushions, and even take time to rip them open."

There is a story that in days of the *Mercury Theater of the Air,* Orson Welles presented a program about Benedict Arnold.

As often happened under the pressures of network production, the dress rehearsal ended only minutes before the show was to go on the air. The stopwatch showed the program was six minutes short. Welles ordered one of his minions to rush down to the network's library and bring him the volume of the *Enclyclopaedia Britannica* which contained a biography of Arnold. This was done; the courier arrived breathless, just as the sweep hand of the clock came around to the hour. Welles went on mike with his usual *voce profondo,* to say, "Good evening, ladies and gentlemen. I am Orson Welles. I have in my hands a copy of the *Encyclopaedia Britannica.* Permit me to read you what this scholarly compendium has to say about the American general and traitor, Benedict Arnold." He then read about 5:50 worth of text, making dramatic emphases, utilizing his flair for histrionic pauses, until enough time had been consumed. Then he ended his impromptu filler with the connective, "Well, so much for what the 14th edition of the *Britannica* has to say about the history of this extraordinary American soldier. Now sit back and listen to *our* version of the story."

The term "cutting room" originated in motion pictures. Up to that time the only cutting rooms were industrial—textiles, steel, paper, produce—and these were generally called departments, not rooms. The doleful expression, "the face on the cutting room floor" obviously referred to the close-up (or to an entire role) that had been snipped out of a picture, and by extension it came to mean anybody unceremoniously dropped from anything. Thus the cutting room became in a sense an operating room where surgery was performed on the body of a movie. Some films were dead on arrival. These may occasionally be seen on late TV.

TV and radio, functioning as they do within tight time modules that must accommodate commercial interruptions, teasers, bumpers, tags and whatnot, obey Procrustes with slavish punctilio. Networks will slice a word in mid-syllable, cut an action in mid-movement, if a program runs beyond the allotted time.

That is why rolling credits at the ends of television programs so often go whizzing past in a blur of names. If you try to follow a name from top to bottom of the tube—that is, if you try to *read* it—you are likely to miss a dozen others. It is a dizzying exercise, almost as frustrating to the viewer as it is to the person who worked hard on the program only to be given public credit in fugitive form, like a streaking raindrop that is promptly liquidated by a windshield wiper.

However, in the matter of vehicles that are not strictly governed by time and space, the benefits of freedom come into play—freedom to explore, expand, round out, penetrate. Such essences have helped to create masterpieces, given the genius of creator and interpreter. But most movies, plays, books or operas will profit by cutting, just as trees do from pruning. Maxwell Perkins, the editor who kept novelist Thomas Wolfe under control, used to cut tens of thousands of words from Wolfe's manuscripts, always with the author's consent. But there stand on the shelves of libraries, and in crowded film vaults, works that go on at boring, fatuous, unmerciful lengths. Of the hundreds of fictional and documentary feature films produced throughout the world every year, at least half of them are too long. The best criterion of overlength is, in most cases, the seat of your pants. If the chair becomes too hard, if you look at your watch, if you wonder about an appointment tomorrow, if you say to yourself "All right already,

I get the point," then the cutter, or the director or producer, whichever of them has the last word, has failed in the faculty of proportion.

There is an old maxim in showbiz—when in doubt, cut. That, too, works only up to a point. If one cuts too deep, blood flows. A work can be vitiated by trims and cuts; it can lose its shape, cohesion and sense; it can die of remedies. Old movies that are trimmed with Procrustean shears to fit TV programming—or cut for reasons of content in that censoring process called bowdlerizing—are nightly shown around the land. When the damage is extensive, they end up as sad sacks of film.

Proportion, like shears and splicers, is the invention of man. Nature is reckless and abandoned in so many ways that it is not to be trusted for models. Even the great spheres themselves are erratic; they blow up into novas, or get desperate and become black holes, all because their furnaces get out of whack. There is delightful symmetry here and there in crystals and blossoms and atomic structures, but in the main, in its massive and prodigal aspects, Nature cares very little about balanced ratios.

Proportion. Sweet proportion. It is one of the glories of all the arts, including the art of living. It could not be otherwise, and still claim the wheel, and the Acropolis, and the face of Helen, and the theorems of Euclid, and the dome of Saint Peter's, and the little rude bridge that arched the flood.

Enough.

BORES

SOMETHING THERE IS THAT DOESN'T LIKE AN 18-foot-high, 24-mile-long nylon fence. Especially when it stretches across hills and dales of unoffending California countryside, uses tons of fabric, 2,050 poles, 100 miles of steel cables, a fleet of trucks, nearly 400 workers, and costs two million dollars to put up and take down.

All of this in the name of art. The art of Christo Javacheff, who is to me one of the supreme bores of our time. He is the same ornamentist who, earlier, had a grand vision which he doggedly realized: He created a mammoth curtain, hundreds of feet wide and almost as deep, and caused it to be raised and suspended across a valley in Colorado. When finally it was tugged, hoisted and winched into place, it looked like the face of a derelict, purposeless dam, flaccid and flapping in a startled breeze. It effectively blotched an otherwise agreeable landscape.

Now if these plastic chefs d'oeuvre were created to advertise
a beer or razor blade, one could at least understand what the
artist was getting at: high visibility. It would be tantamount
to a sort of big-scale land-writing in the style of those flyers
who perform calligraphy all over God's heaven for the glory
of a product. But a sky commercial takes only a single pilot and
a small airplane, and is relatively inexpensive; moreover, the
message is written on the wind and erased in a matter of
minutes.

Not so Christo's advertisements of himself. The media pay
attention to him. Two of the best documentary filmmakers in
the business, Albert and David Maysles, shot a movie around
the hanging of the Colorado drape and called it *Christo's
Valley Curtain*. Like all Maysles pictures it was superbly made
and won Academy honors. As for the nylon fribble of Peta-
luma (the artist himself gave it the Indian-sounding name of
Running Fence), it attracted to the wide outdoors reporters,
cameramen and what one newspaper called "the international
art elite." It also attracted shrill objections from environmen-
talists, the state's attorney general, and a Committee to Stop
the Fence.

Being a stubborn advocate of freedom of expression, I was
glad on principle that Christo won out over these organized
protests and succeeded in unfurling his fence. But none of the
filmed or printed accounts of his exploits explained how Mr.
Javacheff got the millions to organize his expeditionary forces
or pay for the materials and equipment. The question of fund-
ing is not raised idly, for there are at all times hundreds of
worthy projects that seek support—undertakings that have the
potential to encourage talented newcomers, and extend the
work of deserving established artists and performers; there are
prospectuses that beg for help from foundations; ideas that cry

for backers, sponsors, manna-dispensing angels. And among these projects there is always a good chance that something of value to large numbers of people could come of it. Witness the dizzying number of commissioned works of art and music, down through history, which turned out to be of lasting substance.

I confess that I am slow, perhaps retarded, in appreciating the value of Christo's achievements. But I feel under no obligation to applaud a bore, and in my view anyone who asserts himself loudly and continuously without saying anything is constitutionally a bore. What could be louder than two million dollars' worth of obtrusive fabric? Or more continuous than 24 miles of up-and-downhill nylon fence? Or emptier than the whole notion? These mammoth objects are not works of art, but stunts. And as stunts they would be glorious if the valley in Colorado and the hills of Sonoma County were circus grounds. One might just as soon fabricate a colossal peignoir to cover the upper slopes of Mount Whitney, to say nothing of a hood to put over Mount Hood. Why not interpose an enormous Venetian blind between the north and south rims of the Grand Canyon? It would cost only 17 million dollars.

All megalostuntists are essentially bores. I exempt a human salmon like Evel Knievel, because his specialty of hurtling chasms on a motorcycle is gotten over quickly—a fleeting spectacle which can harm nobody but himself; likewise the carnival performer who dives a hundred feet into a rain barrel. But the man who decides he is going to be the first to travel by balloon from Dubuque to Lichtenstein simply generates mass ennui. People properly ask, "What for?" And the idiocy is compounded by the fact that he costs taxpayers a lot of money when the coast guard or the navy has to dispatch planes and ships to go looking for him when he gets lost.

I place Christo not far ahead of the Texan who swallowed 210 live goldfish at one sitting, the Australian who ingested 480 oysters in 60 minutes, and the Yorkshireman who drank three and three-quarters pints of beer while standing upside down. All these Guinness record-holders qualify as conspicuous consumers; and so, of course, does Christo with his acres of polyamide fencing.

Still, I prefer an earnest Christo (all true bores are earnest) to a put-on stuntist like Andy Warhol in his Campbell soup can/Coca Cola bottle/7-cent-airmail-stamp paintings, which come as close to graphic stuttering as you can get outside of the projections of a defective TV tube. It has always been hard for me to decide whether the reiterating glops of Warhol are more tiresome than the art critics who take them seriously. Since Warhol is actually a highly gifted artist, accomplished in many directions and brilliant in some, it is reasonable to suspect that his forays into dullness, such as his hours-long movie of a sleeping man, are simply stunts like swallowing goldfish and curtaining mountain valleys. How serious Warhol was in these exercises only he himself can answer, but I would judge from my experience once as moderator of a panel on which he appeared that he doesn't answer much to anything.

There are distinct echelons of bores. It has been said that some people are so boring that ultimatetly even the grave yawns for them. Personally, I give to Christo and Warhol (who are at least novel in their approach to the efflorescence of bosh) far higher rank than I do the writers, actors, directors and producers of TV's cops-and-robbers-biff-zap-clonk-POW formula-ridden violence programs. Wallpaper designs starring cans and bottles, and nylon arrangements to improve the face of the earth, are after all benign and have a certain dumb

insouciance, whereas the massacres staged on television and
movie screens, the sadism and barbarism transmitted to mass
audiences day after day, are quite something else. They meet
the classic requirement of the bore: they assert themselves
loudly and continuously without saying anything. The wonder
to me is how audiences can take the same bilge over and over
and over. Perhaps what we need in our culture is the capacity
to become bored sooner.

I spoke of Christo and Warhol as being novel in their approach. They are certainly that. It may seem a contradiction
to charge novelty with being dull, but one must never auto-
matically associate newness with sparkle. A numbing example
of this was a Japanese film entered in the Academy Award
foreign film competition a few years back. Some young fire-
brand of a diretcor in Tokyo thought he would try something
absolutely unprecedented: at the beginning and end of every
scene (all interiors) he would occupy the screen with 15 or
20 seconds of empty set *before* and *after* the characters entered
and exited. The first time this happened the audience thought
it was a mistake in editing, but it became clear at the second
intermission that this *mishugas* was by design. Doors, carpets,
wallpaper, drapes, windows, lamps, furniture—you got them
full in the face for what seemed an eternity, every time a scene
started or ended. Precious minutes of your life ticked away
looking at these stupid sets with nobody in them.

Nothing could seem more boringly antic than swallowing
460 oysters in 60 minutes, but somehow, in retrospect, it was
more acceptable than being asked to swallow four Hemingways in 90 minutes. It seems a TV playwright wrote a script
in which Ernest Hemingway was depicted at four different
ages simultaneously, by four different actors, who conversed

with each other as well as with characters who were *not* Hemingway. The concept was fatuous and tedious and so was its execution, but nobody could deny its novelty.

There is a common denominator to bores. They lack a sense of proportion, just as some people are color-blind or tone-deaf. They are in every case excessive: too much yammer, too much nylon, too much film, too many chapters in the novel, too many Hemingways, too many hours of the camera on a sleeping bore, too many beatings, gunshots, chases, too many stunt drivers in too many cars skidding on too many streets, careening on too many mountain roads, leapfrogging over too many obstacles.

However, let's make a constructive suggestion. I suggest that there be an official award to certified bores. It would be a tape of one of the outstanding radio commercials in the history of that art form. In it a choir of heavenly voices keeps chirping at intervals, "Nucoa . . . Nucoa . . . Nucoa . . ." while in the foreground a heavy, deep-toned, flat voice that sounds as though it comes from inside a sepulchre, extols the product. The choir goes on relentlessly singing, "Nucoa . . . Nucoa . . . Nucoa . . ." until, if you are as vulnerable to such stimuli as I am, you are ready to grab the radio set and dunk it in a pail of water, being careful of course to pull the plug out first.

IN PRAISE OF IMAGES

RECENTLY I RETURNED TO THE SCENE OF OC-
cational labors—to a TV control room. Only this time I was
not directing, just watching. Stanley Kramer was at work tap-
ing *The Court Martial of the Tiger of Malaya,* and was de-
ploying cameras with his usual bold hand. Not for him the
cut/ cut/ cut/ cut/ which minces the visualization of most
trials. If a camera was not meant to be moved, I could almost
hear him saying, God would not have given his allegedly favorite species the inspiration for the wheel and the zoom lens.

Anyway, while sitting there before a bank of expensive
electronic hardware, not having to worry about the setup of the
next scene, I was able to enjoy the random play of images on the
monitors, as cameras were positioned and repositioned. This
happens constantly in a TV studio. The eye of the working
camera never blinks unless commanded to do so by a switch on
the control panel. What it sees even while loafing is to the

monitors equally as viable as the most carefully composed shot.

So again, as many times before, I had reason to marvel at the casual beauty of the chance image: the vision of a gavel, a simple gavel, resting on a bench; an extreme closeup of General Yamashita's bespectacled right eye, staring out of the screen like an oriental Cyclops; the nose and lips of a Filipino woman, her face in repose, the features isolated like a detail of a massive sculpture; a brass object, sparkling in a highlight, with the kind of effulgence that Vermeer magically worked into his golds. Thus a wondrous variety of floating accidental pictures, not invariably interesting, but frequently diverting enough to reward looking out for them.

An unforgettable image in my log was one that I saw years ago during the telecast of a routine baseball game. I was lucky enough to be watching at home—it could never have been seen from a seat in the ball park. A batter hit a foul ball which shot back to a high screen behind home plate and ran up the netting toward the camera booth. An alert cameraman pointed his lens at the ball as it soared upward, reached the limit of its energy before gravity took it in train, and for a split second seemed to hover at the point of equilibrium. It came so close to the lens that its stitched seams were clearly legible; it was like a frozen frame of a motion picture. Then it rolled down along the sweeping concavity of the net, and dropped back onto the field. It was for me the best moment of the game—of many games— a pure gift of the gods of the aleatory (which fancy word comes from the Latin for gambler, *aleator*, out of *alea*, a dice game. The aleatory, incidentally, is very big in modern music nowadays, especially among the transistor-loving composers and the Katzenjammer school of John Cage. They just indicate on the score that the musicians are to play whatever comes into their heads. Saves a lot of work for the composer, I imagine.)

Photography is to the layman perhaps the most constantly enticing art. As a buff and follower, at respectful distances, I find myself, like so many others, having the heart of a Stieglitz, with hands that sometimes seem impeded by boxing gloves. I suppose there is in every aficionado the conscious or subconscious yen to participate in the art or sport of his enthusiasm: to approach and touch the medium or object of his admiration. This is a simple enough ambition in the case of the fan who wants to get up close to a movie star, but as it concerns the votary of photography who has no secure knowledge of lenses, filters and speeds, owns no important equipment, and perhaps has neither time nor funds to school himself in the necessities, the situation is more complex.

It is tantalizing to see about one, in the fat infinity of the world, so many restless, ever-changing, inexhaustible prospectuses of photographable stuffs. After all, we walk around with a pair of lenses in our heads, and the best all-purpose cameras yet devised, carrying always in our mysterious lobe of sight the incomparable jiffy-service color lab.

What is exasperating is that one can feel closer to managing the skills of photography than most other arts, and yet be a long hop, skip and delusion away from it. You may love music, yet not be able to go down the street hearing harmonies and melodies; you may love words, yet seldom hear the making of poems or even usable dialogue around you; but the photograph somehow seems always to be there—in the passing old woman, the child hopscotching, the wet pavement, the bleached driftwood, the leaf, the doorknob, the facade of a building, the break of a wave, the cloud, the city, the cat, the ruin, the peak, the wheel, the faces of clocks and clowns.

What fools us is that it seems such an artless art. Just aim,

frame and fire. Ho ho! There is so much more to it that it
boggles. On many levels: information, emotion, esthetics, science. To me one of the wonders of the century, a perfect
marriage of art and science, is a famous photograph made by
Harold Edgerton in 1936. He photographed the splash of a
drop of milk by strobe light. The effect, too fast to be seen by
the sluggish naked eye, is of a perfectly symmetrical white
coronet rising out of a lake of milk, its delicate rays tipped by
globules, some still attached, others floating free. A faint white-
on-white reflection of the coronet appears on the foreground
surface of the milk. The background is black. High up in the
photo, floating like a serene moon, is a pearl-like sphere of
milk, detached, off by itself. I have named it Io; it is too small
to have a longer name.

There are nearly 100 million cameras in service in this
country. New ones sell at a rate of 15 million annually. It has
been figured that some eight billion photographs are taken by
amateurs every year. I suspect most of them are of the baby,
the family, the wedding, the trip. Say half of them cut off
the feet or the head, show pointless bare sky, are underex-
posed or overexposed or blurred. No matter. There would still
be four billion pictures that come out reasonably well, and
among these, there must be millions—all right, tens of thousands—that have some artistic merit. If so, then photography
must be the most widely exercised art in the world. The wonder then is that it is not part of the regular curriculum of
secondary and higher education, like music, poetry and the
graphic arts.

Some still photography is well paid, and I am sure the pro-
fessionals who shoot formal portraits and weddings and convention pictures do all right for themselves, but I was shocked
to learn how many serious photographers, dedicated artists,

§ § § § § § § § § § § § § §

exist on fees that seem barely able to cover their costs in time, equipment and labor. What is worse, most photography agents charge commissions of 40 and 50 percent, which seems to me greedy and confiscatory. Actors, writers, directors, pay no more than 10 percent; why 50 percent for photographers? Maybe the Photo Agents Advisory Board or Guild or Commission or Mafia has some answer: I stand ready to be instructed.

In the meantime, onward and upward with lens and shutter. May all who shoot, all who print film, and all of us who see what comes of it, may the whole population of photography be rewarded with flashes and glimpses of aleatory beauty, with foul balls transformed into kinetic art, and milk drops transmuted to jewelled satellites.

$ELEBRITY

CELEBRITY USED TO BE SOMETHING TO CELE-
brate, but in our time this has been modified. Mainly by the
media. Today celebrity has become a commodity sold routinely
in the market, and used, in turn, to do more selling.

High office means automatic celebrity. Spiro Agnew was a
local wheel in Maryland, but he became national the moment
he was named to be candidate for vice-president in 1968. His
fame grew as he made ringing speeches around the country
and on television, preaching Law & Order, attacking the
media, and deriding what he called nattering nabobs of nega-
tivism. When he was later convicted of a felony, his term in
office ended, but not his celebrity. For although he had the
drab distinction of being the first VP in American history to
plead no contest to a criminal charge, his value as a commodity
only increased.

Playboy magazine paid Agnew a rumored $100,000 for a

novel from his hand. That was quite a good advance for an amateur writer's first novel. Then we were informed by columnist Joyce Haber that Irving (Swifty) Lazar, an agent who earned a reputation in showbiz for making big deals for big clients, was engaged to represent the man who twice picked Agnew as running mate, Mr. Nixon himself. There was no question about Nixon's status as celebrity; neither was there any question in Lazar's mind about the cash value of that celebrity.

Swifty rushed from Paris to San Clemente on receiving a telephone call from Ronald Ziegler, and met with the former president for three hours. According to quotes from Lazar, Nixon "[was] very forthright with me, and from our conversation I believe that he's going to write a historical book that will be one of the biggest best-sellers of all time. I think the [former] president has a great story to tell . . . a remarkable document which contains his version of what happened at the White House to cause Watergate. His side has never been told, and he has a right to tell it."

Nobody has ever disputed that right; it is my impression that Mr. Nixon was persistently invited by investigating committees to tell his side in detail, but he declined.

According to Ms. Haber, the "unstoppable and pugnacious Lazar" got "calls from every publisher"; and within two days of the meeting at San Clemente he decided that an advance payment of $2 million for the book would be contemptibly small. This was by way of commenting on a report that Roger Straus, head of the publishing house of Farrar, Straus, and Giroux, had alluded to a figure of $2 million as "far too high." "That's nonsense," Lazar responded. "I know and like Roger Straus. But you ask a poor man for $2 million and it sounds like a lot of money. You go to a rich man who has $40 million [and ask] for $2 million and it sounds like nothing."

To me it sounds like aggressive agenting, and nobody can fault Mr. Lazar for doing his job unstoppably. What perhaps may be questioned is the avidity with which publishers rush to escalate the wages of crime and the royalties of cover-up.

Mr. Lazar announced that Mr. Nixon's book would be "historical." His mention of history reminded me that Thomas Jefferson died broke. It is a solemn but reasonable supposition that if nineteenth-century media had been as wealthy and diverse as they are today, and if there had been TV to propagate millions of images of the living Jefferson on tubes throughout the land, he would never have had to sell his library at Monticello or put up other of his property for sale in a lottery. One may logically presume, as well, that if media had flourished then as now, Benedict Arnold would have been paid a fortune for his version of what happened; and Aaron Burr would have been offered at least six figures for his account of the duel with Alexander Hamilton.

What Jefferson, Burr and Arnold had in common with Nixon and Agnew was a vast celebrity; what the first three lacked were media that could transform celebrity into sales, and a Lazar to negotiate for them.

The very same VIPs who attacked television, charging abuse, also made use of its willingness to accommodate. There was, for example, no obligation on the part of the TV networks, which Nixon and Agnew badmouthed, to carry Agnew's valedictory address upon being relieved of office; but they did. Whenever Nixon felt he needed a national audience to explain still once more his innocence in the Watergate matter, he was cheerfully afforded cameras and audiences, and no expense was spared by the networks in the form of preempted time and rebates to sponsors for cancelled programs. When Nixon made a festive occasion of his selection of Gerald Ford as vice-president to succeed Agnew, the networks went along and covered the party. Some people felt that all that was required, in the situation, was for the president to submit his choice to Congress in a sealed envelope, the way President Eisenhower might have done. But nobody in TV took that position, and cameras and crews showed up at the White House. Everybody was as pleased as clams at high tide.

Books and periodicals are media too. Far from being hostile to the deposed, these entities will more than take care of the old age of Nixon and Agnew. So, no doubt, will TV.

Happily, the more familiar and channelized activities of commercial celebrity are not related to felonious performance, but instead based on honorable achievement in the arts, sciences and professions. Still, the practice of making salesmen of celebrities has become epidemic. Already aware of the extent to which celebrities had assumed the function of hucksters (Orson Welles for Eastern Airlines, Burgess Meredith for United, star casts touting Pan Am and American, Robert Morley jollifying in behalf of British Airways, Henry Fonda pushing floor wax, Pat Boone peddling milk), I thought perhaps the flood had peaked, but I was wrong. Jill St. John, actress, placed her endearing young charm at the service of an underarm deodorant; Catherine Deneuve and her countrywoman Brigitte Bardot proffered scents and flights, respectively, for Chanel and Air France. Joan Fontaine, whose credits include the movies *Rebecca* and *Jane Eyre*, has spoken in praise of a brand of bread; Patricia Neal for a coffee; Raquel Welch, whose hair is not among her outstanding features, swore publicly by a hair product for brunettes only.

Jack Benny, for whom networks once battled like raging brontosaurs, did insurance and wool commercials. Dustin Hoffman's voice, like that of the turtle, was in our land, but in praise of an automobile; Lee Marvin endorsed a product which acknowledged on its package that it may be hazardous to the health of the purchaser (a cigarette); Julie Newmar was Venus Pomodoro for a tomato cocktail; Sylvia Sidney, whose health I hope is excellent, commended an arthritis remedy; winsome Joe Namath pitched for a popcorn; Burl Ives, minnesinger/actor, pressed, voice-over, for a make of pants; Sammy Davis was right in there for a portable radio; Karl Malden spoke highly, on camera, for American Express; Polly Bergen, in a full-page color advertisement, leaned forward, smiling, over the legend, "A man could never have created Torture." (The product is called "Torture by Polly Bergen." *By*? Does this mean that Polly, herself, worked up the formula in a laboratory from which men were barred?)

On with the show: Sir Laurence Olivier placed a lifetime of performing experience at the disposal of Polaroid. Fred Clark was barker for a dog food; Don Wilson spoke for regularity through a laxative; Richard Conte's embassy was in the name of a breath mint; Fred MacMurray was the voice and face of Greyhound Bus; George Montgomery pledged the efficacy of a furniture polish; Neil Armstrong, the first man to put a boot down on the surface of the moon, did a commercial for a banking association. (A small step for the banking association; a giant step down for Neil Armstrong.)

I suppose there is a kind of reciprocity at work in all this. Celebrities are made by the media, and, being the sons and daughters of television, having been sent out in the world by it with money in pocket, they have no objection to doing commercials for the dear old girl, especially if they are well paid for it. Aeschylus, Milton, Gandhi and those sacred sisters, the Muses, might find it hard to understand, but to Swifty Lazar it is all very clear, and that is what counts in the society of the big sell.

CAN THE LAUGHTER

MIRTH THAT WAS DUBBED LAST WEEK HATH present laughter and future reruns, and is audible on TV daily. There are chuckles at fitted intervals, giggles by the metered foot, small jollity, medium jollity, jumbo jollity, graded like olives, and all fed into the sound track by a solemn man who is paid by the hour for sitting at the console of a laugh machine and pressing keys.

Canned laughter is a form of self-praise. It has the advantage over external praise of being able to be laid on thickly in the right places. Since genuine laughter is a sign of approval of the joke, or at the very least amused acceptance, television sees to it that none of its comedy is disapproved or unreceipted, by supplying prefabricated approbation along with the product. It is a little like holding an election in which there is only one candidate, and if you don't choose to cast a ballot it will be done for you. All nicely taken care of by management.

Like a roisterer who has picked up bad habits along with a disease or two in the course of brash careering, TV has taken over some of the worst conventions of radio, and added to them. Perhaps chief of these is the studio warm-up. It is unthinkable that an audience at a stage play, or a movie, would be worked on by a pitchman in advance of the opening curtain or fade-in. Spectators in a movie house would pelt a screen with insults, if not popcorn or harder missiles, if the sound track dared to simulate audience laughter; in other words, if it presumed to do the work of perceiving, digesting and enjoying comedy for the customers in their seats. Yet this is what happens routinely in television production.

The warm-up of a studio audience is just as much an exercise of wheedling and coaxing as the commercials that follow in due time. The latter are designed to reduce sales resistance; the former, to reduce laugh resistance. The bodies who fill the chairs in studios are living applause machines. They are not trusted by the producers to respond properly without priming, nor to applaud spontaneously. Hence the ceremony of holding up APPLAUSE cards. It works. The good people are happy to oblige, probably because they have paid no admission charge, are guests of the program, and thus feel it only cricket to take such orders as Start Applause, Continue Applause, Stop Applause.

The phrase *deus ex machina*, literally a god from a machine, originally alluded to the practice in classical tragedy of bringing on a god by stage machinery to solve superhuman problems. But in mechanized TV comedy, the god *is* the machine, and is brought on to solve piddling problems such as what to do with a bare patch of tape when the humor is so thin that it must be covered with a noise of some kind, preferably laughter. A measure of the inanity of the average synthesized chuckle is the annoyance you feel when, as you are watching a program, there is even the slightest dubbed titter at a speech or movement which would not under normal circumstances produce anything more audible than a yawn. Sometimes even a gesture, like the lifting of a hand in mock protest, is scored for cackles.

"Did you put the cat out?" asks the husband.

"Yes. And it objected," replied the wife.

"It did?"

"Sure. It felt put out."

Whether or not anybody in the great unseen audience of broadcasting thinks that is funny, and there are solid grounds for doubting it, instant and appreciative laughter is dubbed in, registering between 2 and 4 on the Beaufort scale. It is all part of the grand machinization which is supposed somehow to improve the quality of life. Dial a prayer. Pick out a sentiment in the catalog of numbered greetings sendable by telegram, and you will be spared the pangs of composition. Drop a coin in the slot, pull a lever, and if the god in the one-armed-bandit likes you, the jackpot is yours. Speak the truth into a detecting machine, and absolve yourself.

There is a ripple effect to all this. Even an actor who might be expected to prefer live performance on a legitimate stage over a remote, motor-driven reproduction of his role, may opt for hardware. He may discover that he has been indoctrinated, or in a sense drugged, by machine and, in the process, alienated from live audiences.

One of my favorite actors and people is William Conrad, whose talents far surpass the requirements of his *Cannon* series on television. But he gave me a turn when he announced that he would never again appear in a stage play after his experience in *That Championship Season*. He told a reporter in Chicago, "I can't wait for the last performance. In TV or films, you do a scene, you think it's good, and you say, 'All right, print it.' Last night the play was perfect. Everything was great. So why bother to do it again tonight?"

"But how about the excitement of appearing before an audience?" he was asked.

"I'm not even aware the audience is there," he answered, "even though some of them are as close to me as I am to you" (across a table).

Alas, it is a case in point. It would seem that Mr. Conrad is so accustomed to performing before machines—the cameras and mikes of TV and film production—that he has lost the apperception of live spectators, whose presence sometimes gives as much as it gets from the artist. His choice is a circle of apparatus. But suppose Jascha Heifetz or Beverly Sills or Vladimir Horowitz or, for that matter, Elton John, each decided, after a "perfect performance," to forsake the concert stage because everything was so great in the last appearance there was no point in bothering to do it again. All of these artists are available on mechanical devices (LPs, tapes, films) and their recordings are capable of unlimited repeats and reruns. But still they persist in giving fresh live performances. It may be argued that they persist because the money is good, but that argument does not hold up. The money is also good for actors in hit stage plays. Often they are carried over into the television and movie versions, as was the case, for example, with Yul Brynner in *The King and I*. Such fallout can be especially lucrative.

I imply nothing lesser or inferior in the nature of mechanized arts like film and TV. They can be, and often have been, worthy carriers of high art. But it is at time demeaning to both vehicles and artists for parties to prepare an audience beforehand by tenderizing it, by clowning right up to air time, by wooing, drilling or instructing spectators in a manual of reception. It amounts to organizing and staging praise for one's product before it is even presented.

Television has revived the claque. (The word is out of the French *claqueur,* to clap, and its history is tied up with the theater. In France, at one time, managements employed permanent bodies of professional clappers. The profession spread abroad, and claques became particularly conspicuous in opera houses, where indeed they flourish to this day. You can hear them bawling bravos from La Scala to Sydney.)

TV claques are of two kinds: the voluntary and the hired. The first is the studio audience, recruited from God knows where. It responds on cue, and its semirobotized cheering and whistling take on the proportions of ovation. The second is the laugh-maker, a one-man electronic claque which contributes to the recipe of the program, artificial flavoring. The process is actually called "sweetening."

Yet whatever has been said about the institution of the claque, it is not nearly as withering as the cool definitions given by standard dictionaries that are famous for not making moral judgments. "Claque, n.—Any body of truckling applauders," says one. "Any group of persons," says another, "who bestow praise out of motives of self-interest . . . a group of sycophants."

While these terms may be too extreme to describe the sometimes spontaneous or genuinely appreciative studio audience, there can be no question that the *principle* of claquerie (don't look it up, it's coined) is guilty as charged, even though the audience itself may be innocent of motives of self-interest. In the case of canned laughter, if I ever found myself on a tribunal judging it, I would be a stern magistrate. The minimum sentence would be five years at the hard labor of digging old jokes out of Joe Miller's mine.

FIRE, BLOOD, PASSION

THE SAME REDOUBTABLE GEORGE C. SCOTT
who rejected an Academy Award for acting is on record as saying that American actors are better than their English kith at
playing Shakespeare. The latter, he would have us understand,
have refined their playing so much that "they've taken the
fire, the blood, the passion out of it. They've turned Shakespeare into an elocution class. I think American actors put the
fire, the blood and the passion back into it—it may not be
beautiful, but damn it, it sure is exciting!"

I think Mr. Scott is as wrong about this as he was about
The Savage Is Loose, the film for which he acted, directed
and fought with rating boards. He cannot have seen Peter
Brook's all-English production of *A Midsummer Night's
Dream*, which had the energy of an atomic pile; nor can he have
seen Olivier, Genn, McKern, Gielgud, Hemmings, Glenda
Jackson, the Redgraves, Peggy Ashcroft, Ralph Richardson,

Alec Guinness—oh, a hundred superb Britons in royal flush after royal flush (usually to full houses) of Shakespearean roles. Nor can he have watched the BBC's television productions.

Alas, American actors only rarely have a sense of heightened language. They are embarrassed before the sweep and flourish of Elizabethan verse, and awkwardly self-conscious in the presence of stately periods. There is little call for panache in group systems like The Method, where actors are taught awed obedience to directors but only secondary respect for the nuances of language, the richness of its texture, its musicality and grace. The dispensable element, as Mr. Scott so bluntly puts it, is beauty.

The last people to whom I would entrust an actor for Shakespearean training are the methodologists who cling to systematic dogmas. I got the impression, from watching one such guru work with actors on scenes from a tragedy, that Shakespeare's meaning was not nearly as important as what might be going on in the actor's sense memory. One must be almost impregnable to the purport of the master not to take direct cues from Shakespeare himself, as set down in the speech to the players:

"Speak the speech I pray you, as I pronounced it to you, trippingly on the tongue; but if you mouth it, as many of your players do, I had as lief a town-crier spoke my lines. Nor do not saw the air too much with your hand, thus; but use all gently: for in the very torrent, tempest, and—as I may say— whirlwind of passion, you must acquire and beget a temperance, that may give it some smoothness."

It offended Hamlet to hear a robustious actor "tear a passion to tatters, to very rags." What Shakespeare thought fitting to the interpretation of verse has always been good enough for me, and I should like to think that many others in the media consider this bit of coaching from the author to be valid even in this hyperkinetic era.

But Mr. Scott is not alone in the primacy he gives to what he calls fire, blood and passion. Most of the TV and film industries subscribe to the same attitude. Muscle! Action! Blood! Especially blood! Erik Barnouw, in his volume *The Image Empire,* quotes a memo from producer Quinn Martin to an assistant: "I wish you would come up with a different device than running the man down with a car, as we have done this now in three different shows. I like the idea of sadism, but I hope we can come up with another approach to it." In that formula we see the prescription filled: passion, blood and fire. Not beautiful, but exciting.

It is not as though Shakespeare wanted his stage to be static. In the same shoptalk to the players, he has Hamlet advising them, "Be not too tame, either, but let your own discretion be your tutor; suit the action to the word, the word to the action; with this special observance, that you o'erstep not the modesty of nature." Well, thank you, Hamlet, but nature's modesty is given scant shrift in all but a few precincts of TV, and not very much more in films and theater. With numbing regularity, TV brings us routinized violence, obligatory scenes of mayhem, and shoot-outs in which the action is suited to the format of the show, never to the word.

Mr. Scott is an excellent actor, if not always a refined director, and it is disappointing that his talents as the former do not make clear to him that there is a difference between what he dismisses as "elocution," and speech delivered with special observance of the sense of words and the beauty of language. But then Mr. Scott and others of us are victims of a long process of desensitization to poetry which may be traced perhaps to deficiencies in our educational values.

The United States is not a safe place for poetry. The editors of *Time*, in a preface to an anthology of modern American verse, wrote, "In a country where only half the adults read one book of any kind a year, the poet is virtually ignored; his books sell badly and usually at a loss to the publisher; his readers sometimes number not many more than the sum total of his fellow poets and their students." No wonder Americans do poorly with verse drama. I do not say we are all slobs when it comes to Elizabethan theater. There have been occasional fine productions and splendid individual performances. But in the long run, we are one of the underdeveloped nations when it comes to Shakespeare.

As a people, as a culture, we have become so alienated from poetry that whenever a playwright has the pluck to raise his language above the colloquial, or goes beyond the permissible tolerances of smooth, witty, "sophisticated" expression, the effect vexes many of our critics just as Shakespeare's eloquence confounds many of our actors and directors.

Cartwheels and somersaults are circus stuff; shrieking, yelling and hand-sawing are for a marketplace in Tunis; mouthing and mumbling are for theoreticians arousing themselves from the torpors of self-analysis as they probe for the shimmering truth of why they should get up from a chair in a scene. None of this is for Shakespeare.

Enjoyment of the sessions of sweet silent thought does not prejudice movement. Action can indeed be exciting, as all football fans know; and the Chase, an honorable dramatic device, merits the long run it has enjoyed. But excitement can also stand quietly. Conflicts of the heart, mind and spirit can be as fierce as the battles of armies. The grand confrontations between man and God that occur in the Bible, have at least as much fire power as *SWAT* or *Mod Squad*. If the funeral

oration of Pericles was elocutionary, then let us open schools of
elocution.

There can be no question about the rating positions of fire,
blood and passion. The popularity of entertainment that rests
on these piers is measurably greater than that of contemplative
works; still, that is no reason why Trendex leaders should be
considered superior. Rod McKuen will always outsell Robert
Frost.

In this time when minority rights are high in our consciousness, perhaps we should give more thought to cultural discrim-
ination. The absence from our lives of serious poetry is so
chronic and accustomed that nobody pays it much heed; but
there are many more millions of music lovers than there are
poetry buffs across the land, and they *do* notice the squeeze
on classical music. Radio stations that once carried full sched-
ules of classics have either expired or reduced their quotients;
now there are just a few. They are in the way of becoming an
extinct species.

A measure of this shrinkage may be seen in a compilation
made by the Datsun Travel Guide for motorists. It listed the
kind of music broadcast by 196 radio channels in 48 states and
the District of Columbia. There were 42 stations playing only
folk, or jazz, or progressive, or country, or black, or soul. There
were 146 stations playing only rock. Now guess the number of
stations playing only classical music, among the 196 surveyed.
You guessed it. Zero.

But to get back to the claim that our actors are better at
Shakespeare than the English: Before we beat our chests,
George, over how much more talented we are than the people
of other countries, let us make sure we have a supportable case.
So far, I feel safe in bragging only about our plumbers, free-
way engineers and shortstops.

O DEATH,
WHERE IS THY YUK?

YEARS AGO ALFRED HITCHCOCK MADE A FILM named *The Trouble with Harry*, whose comic invention con-consisted of a corpse loosely disposed, for most of the picture, in various parts of a house. Since corpses are not amusing to begin with, and tend to become less jolly with each passing day, the comedy was, to put it mildly, strained. It was a surprisingly bad picture from a master of the medium, and I hoped that its example would deter others from similar dalliance with what is the proper study of undertakers.

But no: a few years later there came *The Loved One*, which was Tony Richardson's worst picture and managed to offend everybody with agile impartiality. It dealt with mortuaries, stiffs, embalming and cemeteries, and it enrolled Jonathan Winters, among other actors of proven comic proficiency, in its cast. This film, like *The Trouble with Harry*, was somewhat less hilarious than the average funeral.

And then came *Avanti,* from the hugely talented Billy Wilder, which offers a morgue with a fine view of the landscape of Ischia, and presents much ado, for reel after reel, about two coffins holding the remains of aging lovers who died in an auto crash. I hope I will not spoil the ending for those who have not yet seen *Avanti,* by disclosing that it involves a third corpse, ensconced in a sealed coffin, soaring off on the blades of a helicopter into what, in about two hours, will no doubt be a sunset.

Ghoulish humor, like any other kind, depends on the art, or at least the taste, with which it is executed. The gravediggers in *Hamlet* sing and jest as they prepare for the internment of Ophelia, but their sport is not at the expense of the dead lady; the talk is wryly legalistic and spiked with conundrums. Even so, Hamlet, coming upon them, is offended:

Hamlet: *Hath this fellow no feeling of his business, that he sings at grave-making?*

Horatio: *Custom hath made it in him a property of easiness.*

Hamlet: *Tis e'en so; the hand of the little employment hath the daintier sense.*

The trouble with *The Trouble with Harry* and similar works in whatever medium, is that the japes on death come not from professional gravediggers in whom custom has made easy the burial of mortal remains, but from professed entertainers, who, not being regularly employed in the properties of embalming and cremation, should, according to Hamlet's comment, have a daintier sense. Alas, they do not.

A whole issue of *National Lampoon,* which bills itself as "The Humor Magazine," was devoted to death. Among its contents are three pages of cartoons on *Telling a Kid His Parents Are Dead.* In one a minister is saying to a little tad as they walk through a park, "And that's why God threw your parents in front of a subway car."

Another section fantasizes on the benefits of freezing and storing human cadavers. In one drawing two happy parents sit over a birthday cake, father blowing a horn, mother twirling a noisemaker, both wearing party hats; between them stands the blue-faced corpse of their child, removed from the freezer for the celebration. The legend explains that "the doting parents of a departed child" could console themselves by holding repeated birthday anniversaries down through the years (obviously it would be the same birthday each year, since a dead child does not normally grow older).

So far this humor seems to me elusive, but at least it is impersonal. Deeper into the same issue of *National Lampoon*, however, several identified persons are made the object of death jokes. In a parody on *Playboy* called *Playdead*, there is a takeoff on the *Playboy* Interview format. Dan Blocker of the TV *Bonanza* series, who died late in 1972, is asked several questions by a *Playdead* interviewer. No answers appear—the spaces are left blank. (Cute, see?)

Two editors of *Playboy* who died in the same year as Dan Blocker are likewise given *Lampoon*'s special attention on a page entitled *Under the Lawn*. Accompanying their actual names are photographs—next to the name of A. C. Spectorsky, editorial director, is a shot of the feet of an ostensibly dead man, visible through a door left ajar; next to the name of Ken Purdy (described as an "auto maniac" since he wrote about automobiles) is a picture of an empty boot hanging from the door handle of a limousine. The text on Purdy reads, in part:

"In the period of time prior to Ken's personal blowout, Ken liked to hike . . . and bake bread. 'Doing things like that . . .

makes me feel I'm getting back to the earth.' Ken went back
to the earth for good this past June and seems to be enjoying
it, from what we can gather. Always one for relaxing *au
naturel* in his father's funeral parlor, Ken . . . ."

It is part of a melancholy syndrome of our time that death,
and indeed suffering, are too often viewed with the callousness
one would expect from a social order of insects. The astronomical scale of wholesale death has insensitized many of us:
millions killed in wars, millions exterminated in concentration
camps, hundreds of thousands slaughtered and maimed on the
highways of the world every year. The avenues of violence
are widening: snipers, bomb-throwers, hijackers; assassins in
Memphis, Belfast, Munich, Dallas, Los Angeles, Tel Aviv,
New Orleans. Murdered: a President, a senator, a Nobel
laureate, a labor leader. Crippled for life: a governor. Gunned
down: unarmed Asian civilians. Bombed: hospitals. Tortured,
stabbed, mangled: Sharon Tate and friends, and clusters of
others.

Where does it end? Not in the streets, certainly. Not on
hotel roofs. Not on campus towers. Not on the TV tube. Not
on the wide screen. Television affords us, week in and week
out, regular seminars on violence: each spy, detective and
western episode has its obligatory melee, its fists, knives and
guns. The volume of blood spilled in the combined movies of
Sam Peckinpah would be enough to supply twenty remakes
of *The Godfather*.

An excellently made documentary film named *Manson*,
based on the background of the savage Tate-LaBianca murders, is hackle-raising in its disclosure of the *attitudes* of aficionados toward murder. Grisly as the actual killings were, they
are less shocking than the cold, knowing, unhesitating endorse-
ment of butchery by adherents to the Manson philosophy, if

that term may be used. One girl, who looks as wholesome as a 4-H maid, faces squarely into the lens, fondles a deadly hooked knife, runs a finger lovingly over its blade, and speaks of the pleasures of blood-letting, and of how terrific it would be· to flourish this weapon in the dark. Another speaks of enjoying the sight of a severed human head, rolling around on a floor.

If life is cheap on the tube and screen, and body counts are routine in war news, and the dead become just so many inert clowns, is it so surprising that a carload of boys can careen down a street and casually shoot dead a little girl standing outside her home? It happened.

One need attach no false reverence to death for the sake of death, but I think it might not be out of order to propose that, if only for sweet experiment's sake, there be a voluntary moratorium on necro-comedy in all media. Perhaps, with a modest beginning, there might in time be a downtrend instead of an uptrend in senseless killings, and in the relish and humor derived from them.

Let us, for God's sake and our own, permit the dead to rest in peace.

HOUSES OF ART

THERE IS SOMETHING TO BE SAID FOR THE good small museum as against a Grand Central Station of art, and I beg leave to say it. It is the difference between a satisfying and nourishing meal, and Trimalchio's bulging board.

Vastness is oppressive when thrust on human senses and capacities. The pyramids of antiquity, the mammoth heads of Abu Simbel and Mount Rushmore, are meant to be seen from afar, not touched. Similarly one can no more feel intimate with a wing of paintings in the Louvre than with the north shore of Lake Superior.

No matter how disciplined we are about limiting ourselves to a particular suite or section of a huge museum, there is always a threat of surfeit. Even to *get* to the chosen area, you must pass through the Egyptian or Greek or Melanesian quarter, and it seems almost a misdemeanor to proceed briskly, just for passage, through any forest of treasures.

The massiveness of a major museum can be intimidating. The truth is, there is no grace to bulk, except when reduced to a postcard view of Mont Blanc, or in seeing the *Queen Elizabeth 2* from another ship a mile away. Of course, it is comforting to know that the Metropolitan and the British museums exist; like Everest, they attract because they are *there*—but that is not the same as saying that one can visit them comfortably, or digest their intensely rich and varied fare without sometimes feeling like the man in the Alka-Seltzer commercial who groans, "I ate the whole thing!"

A day in the dimly lit Prado or the draughty Hermitage may grandly reward the art lover by sheer profusion of masterpieces, but the experience is qualitatively different from an afternoon spent in a relatively modest ambience like that of The Phillips Gallery in Washington, D.C. Here, in a four-story, turn-of-the-century house of brownstone and red brick, paintings and sculpture are not displayed as archival objects but are given a home. The collection is eclectic enough to satisfy the most roving tastes, yet it specializes, too: For example, it has the largest group of Bonnards in this country, perhaps in the world. It has three very important Cézannes; one Goya; a few fabled Van Goghs; a fine cluster of Klees, some Dufy, Winslow Homer, Ben Nicholson. Renoir's generous *The Luncheon of the Boating Party* is handsomely situated, as is proper to its fame and luminousness, a radiance that lifts the heart as much as it lights up the room.

The National Gallery in the same city is glorious but chaste by compare; there is an immaculateness about it that is a little chilling. A painting on its walls, or in any such official terminal of art, wears something of the hauteur of its surroundings. It looks down at rather than across to you. The same painting in the Phillips, or the Huntington Art Gallery in San Marino, or the Clark Art Institute in Williamstown, Massachusetts, or in a bijou of a museum in Chapel Hill, North Carolina, would ask after your health, and invite you to sit for a bit of communion. There are upholstered chairs, with backs, in the Phillips, not for show but to be sat in: It reminds you of those few public parks where the signs say, "Please walk on the grass."

A singularly graceless if not uncouth phrase in current usage is "blow the mind." It is intended to describe anything from an acid trip to a legitimately edifying amazement. Well, the danger of a titanic museum is that it tends to blow the mind, to boggle the perception, to blur the vision. The growth of a great museum, like that of a great city, should not be unchecked. That way lies elephantiasis. Enough is enough. Three-ring circuses are truly gross organisms: Spectators are not lizards with turreted eyes that move independently of each other. And if any of us had three eyes, we would be *in* the circus, not watching it.

It is a token of the good health of our culture, that masses throng to the big museums, especially on weekends or when there is a special show. The Metropolitan Museum is now New York's number one tourist attraction. The *Impressionist Epoch* exhibition drew more than a half-million people at a rate of 1,500 per hour. Some years ago a mighty Van Gogh exhibition at the same stand attracted more paid admissions than a vintage year Notre Dame football team playing in Yankee Stadium on the same day. But an art museum is not a ball park, and it is barbaric to view the work of a master while being jostled in a long, shifting line of people. I prefer to go on a rainy day, or come early or late, or at any unlikely hour, so that I may stand before a painting for a whole minute, or until closing time if I so wish, without being borne off on an inexorable human tide.

Another product of hypertrophy in museums is the individual electronic guide, the prerecorded voice-over which explains as you go along. The Hirshhorn Museum of the Smithsonian has a Telesonic instrument which one holds to the ear. The only trouble with it, and other systems of the same type, is that the sound leaks if the device is not pressed tightly to the head. As a result there are wisps and scraps of audible information about paintings that you have long passed, or not yet reached, which come at you while you are trying to concentrate on the canvas of your own choice.

The Hirshhorn is big enough to come within the compass of too-big, but it has an airiness and proportion that make it less oppressively weighty than most of the giants. One may emerge from the Hirshhorn reeling slightly, but not stooped by the tonnage of what one has seen. Moreover there is a spunky spirit about the place; it invites you to have fun as no other art museum I know. The key is struck in an amusing sign displayed on every level of the building, which reads:

IN THE MUSEUM . . .
PLEASE . . . MUSE, CONVERSE, SMOKE,
STUDY, STROLL, TOUCH, ENJOY,
LITTER, RELAX, EAT, LOOK,
LEARN. . . .

However, the words SMOKE, TOUCH, LITTER and EAT are crossed out with red X's. There is nothing stuffy about either the form of that request or the collection itself, which seems to have been based on one man's enthusiasms rather than the criteria and expertise of a panel of savants. The museum thus speaks a loose *lingua franca* of art rather than strict Pedaguese or Educanto, and that seems to me all right, for a change, in a world where not everybody is Bernard Berenson or Kenneth Clark.

Incidentally, on the top floor of the Hirshhorn hangs a painting by Edward Ruscha entitled *The Burning of the Los Angeles County Art Museum*. It is a very literal rendering of the building on Wilshire Boulevard, as it might be seen from a high rise across the way. No people are about, nor any traffic; in the solid gray-blue sky and background there is no more atmosphere than you find in a blueprint. But thick smoke and flames are pouring from the northwest wing of the museum. What pique Mr. Ruscha may have against Los Angeles's finest, or why; or what bad cess he may wish the institution, are not explained, and I did not have time to inquire of Mr. Ruscha, Mr. Hirshhorn or Harry Smithsonian. Nevertheless, I cheer the restraint of the dignified Angelines of the county museum in not retorting through a commissioned sculpture entitled *Earthquake Rocking the Hirshhorn Museum,* to be displayed in the very wing gutted by Mr. Ruscha in his painting.

Among depots of culture, there is only one variety that cannot possibly be too big, and that is a major library. After all, there can never be too many books, nor too many copies of particular titles, considering that earnestly sought volumes have a way of being out on loan when you need them most. With respect to size, there is a statistical anomaly that broods over the superb Research Library on the campus of UCLA. The library is excellent in every way that one can be: It catalogs about three million books and periodicals for the benefit of 30,000 students and 2,000 faculty members. But there are exactly 23 metered parking spaces in the lot closest to the building. It costs 25 cents to park in one of these spaces—not for an hour, not for 45 minutes, but for 37½ minutes. Not since Fellini's movie entitled 8½ has a simple fraction been given such distinction in a cultural context.

THE POOR
ARISTOCRATS

A SCRAPPY AND VALUABLE CITIZEN OF THE RE-
public of music is Henri Temianka, conductor-violinist, whose
attitude toward the enemies of culture is that of a hungry
wolverine going after a polecat. He coined a slogan for his
Chamber Music Society: "Aristocratic art in a democratic
society." It is a good slogan up to a point, because it appeals to
the snob in each of us. But beyond that point it runs into
hazards.

One of these hazards is the common misconception of
chamber music: that it is very special, and not for most people.
That is like saying that superior painting, as opposed to calen-
dar art and commercial illustration, is likewise not for the
majority. If we went by this formula, there would be no
Louvre, no Prado, no Metropolitan Museum. Paintings would
hang only on the walls of the Rockefellers, the Onassii, and

Norton Simon. But go to any of the big museums of a Sunday. You will meet and be jostled by the electorate.

I have heard it argued that the serious composer does not write for the herd, but for a special coterie. It may seem that way, but I have never yet met a composer who deliberately set out not to be heard by people. If that is his goal, he can always bury his score as a dog does a bone, and wait for someone to sniff it out.

If a composer is rash enough to be committed to serious music, to spend his time writing symphonies, concertos and chamber music, then, to the broad public, I am afraid he is a kind of dedicated kook. In a nice way, of course. He is admissible to dinner parties and symposia on music, and may serve on college faculties and all that. He could possibly make a living writing movie scores or TV commercials, but he is not expected to support himself by writing the aristocratic music for which Mr. Temianka is sloganeer.

A composer friend of mine once wrote a violin concerto for Mr. Heifetz. He worked on it for two or three years. I don't know what his arrangement was with Jascha Heifetz, beyond the honor of a public performance by the maestro, but I do know what he was paid in the way of royalties for later performances by the New York Philharmonic and the Dallas Symphony orchestras. His fee in New York City, money capital of the world, was $50. In Dallas, where they are big spenders, his fee was $75.

Another composer friend, a distinguished man of many credits, wrote an opera. He worked on it through two marriages, and spent thousands of dollars of his own money having the score copied and bound. The opera was hailed by Stokowski and Barbirolli, good jurors both; but in 30 years the opera has never come near production.

So what incentive is there for a practicing composer to write serious new works? He may wait 30 years for a performance, or have none at all. The appreciation of posterity makes mighty thin soup, assuming posterity will ever be interested at all.

I believe a man who has and exercises a rare, but not especially marketable, talent is a national treasure, and should be treated as such. He is entitled to support by the people and for the people. Certain societies have long felt that way about their poets, painters, playwrights, composers. The Finns supported Sibelius; Pope Julian supported Michelangelo; the Borgias took care of Leonardo; the Russians saw that Shostakovich and Katchaturian got plenty of central heating in their apartments in the winter. The old poet-laureateship of England was an acknowledgment of this principle, and so is the Old Vic.

There has been a happy history of rich giving; both the donor and the artist have been, for the most part, more than satisfied. In a poem *To Rich Givers,* Walt Whitman says:

> *What you give me, I cheerfully accept.*
> *A little sustenance, a hut and garden, a little money as I rendezvous with my poems.*
> *Why should I be ashamed to own such gifts? . . .*
> *For I myself am not one who bestows nothing upon man and woman. . . .*
> *I bestow upon any man or woman the entrance to all the gifts of the universe.*

That is certainly a serene view, but Mr. Whitman is right, so long as there are givers and they do not insist on controlling the copy. But creative men are human, too; and while it is nice to be endowed, they would rather not be objects of charity. Whitman, notwithstanding his sentiment about rich givers, supported himself at a clerical job; Keats was a surgical assistant; Gauguin pasted billboards for a time; Rousseau, Melville and Hawthorne had jobs in the customs service; Borodin was a chemist; Robert Burns a tax collector.

Today many artists stay solvent only through teaching, by writing criticism, or by doing odd jobs of journalism or journey-manism. It is staggering to think how much more artistic treasure the world might have today, if the greatest of its talents could have devoted their full time and energy to the work they were clearly intended to do, and wanted to do.

Yet it seems to me there is at least one way in which the artist can be rewarded without being patronized, and that is the commissioned work. If federal subsidy is cried down as coddling, then let the commissioning be done by entities whose responsibility and public obligation it is to encourage, stimulate and sponsor new works. First there are the television networks, whose charters to function are not theirs by divine right, but by federal commitment to serve "the public interest and necessity." They have lots of money to throw around, and they do throw it around. (One of them paid its president an annual salary of $124,000, plus a $100,000 bonus, plus stock options, plus an unlimited expense account, plus a limousine with chauffeur, plus retirement fund advantages, and sever-ance pay, when he left, amounting to a quarter of a million dollars.)

This load did not stagger the network; it still made $40 million after taxes that year, and that is splendid. But could it not, somewhere out of all that fortune, have put aside a few thousands to commission a new string quartet or a concerto that might even—who knows—have outlasted the current TV season—and to hell with ratings for that hour?

It is not hard to commission anything, if you have the funds. It's as easy as picking up the telephone. (I did it myself once, in behalf of a big organization; the composer was Aaron Copland.) It would seem to me that any network which can spend $200,000, or twice that much, on a TV pilot that may never get on the air, might also consider investing in a new work by a deserving composer. The late Ernest Bloch, and before him, Béla Bartók—both needy cases—might have left us still more imperishable works, if they had had that kind of support. Many memorable and lasting things have come from commissions, and have redounded to the glory of the commissioner. To some Medicis it has been their only claim to lasting notice—take Rasoumovsky and Esterhazy.

What matters, finally, is our outlook on the aristocratic arts. It would be nice if we could see the day when those who write serious music and those who play it, can take their place among the living assets of the country, as much entitled to the dignity of their occupations and to basic security, as astronauts, teamsters, advertising men, ministers, insurance executives and realtors. When that time comes, all of us may be very senior citizens, but even so it would be pleasant just to sit and listen.

ET TU, DALI

THE WINGS OF MAN. A NOBLE PHRASE. IT
could be the title of a definitive history of aviation, from Icarus
to the supersonic. It could be, but is not. It is the tag end of a
radio commercial for Eastern Airlines, spoken by Orson Welles
in his lushest mezza voce. As read by the master, the line has
poetic thrust, as though it were the payload of a soliloquy from
one of the great plays. The inference is that when you fly
Eastern, even though your trip is from Newark to Philadelphia, you are somehow participating in a hallowed rite of
civilization.

United Airlines, on the other hand, is down to earth. "After
your full breakfast," says Burgess Meredith, "we roll out the
salami." He speaks anonymously in this commercial, but there
is no mistaking his lyrical style, which trembles on the verge
of transcending into song. Meredith deserves better than having to promise salami in a brief public utterance.

Pan American World Airways had the benefit of Lee J. Cobb, also recorded anonymously, but his voice was instantly identifiable by devotees of theater, films and TV. He brought to this commercial the substantiality of his mature judgeships, the gravity of his western marshals and board chairmen. (Gravity is useful to airlines.)

Robert Morley, English bon vivant and actor, is, in the Jungian sense, the persona of BOAC. His extraordinarily mobile face suggests a jolly good flight, fine eating, and witty fellow passengers with funds of rollicking anecdotes. The fares, however, are roughly the same as those of competing airlines.

Chet Huntley's commercials for American Airlines were Jeffersonian in dignity, and among a series of statements undamaging to the reputation of that carrier, he referred to certain of AA's fleet of aircraft as "an inspiration for airplanes yet to be built."

So celebrities have moved in force into commercials, both voice-over, front-facing, sitting, standing, acted-out, anonymous and nonymous. And I was very sorry to see it happen. On several grounds. First, it sustains the old snob advertising precept that the glamour or fame of a spokesman counts as much as, if not more than, the merit of the product. I am not myself persuaded to fly Pan American because Joan Crawford, on camera, said she had trust in the experience of that airline. What persuades me to fly Pan Am, or any other airline, is whether it flies to the city I am headed for, at the time I want to go, and whether my previous trips on the line have been satisfactory. The fact that Eastern is, as Orson Welles assures us, the second largest airline in the free world, is less important to me than the circumstance that its wings of man can get me from Boston to Raleigh, North Carolina, without hav-to change planes.

I would rather not sit next to a jolly passenger on a flight to London, thanks just the same to Robert Morley. I might prefer to read, or write, or sleep. It is sometimes difficult or impossible to turn off a gabby extroverted neighbor in full flight.

But aside from the triviality, to me, of celebrity endorsements, there is an economic factor. Most celebrities, by dint of the achievements that established their fame, are well off. Most little-knowns are not. There are hundreds of unemployed or seldom-used actors who could make anonymous radio or voice-over commercials just as effectively. I do not blame stars for picking up easy income from commercials when other work is slow, but there is something peculiar to me about a superstar huckstering for a product when he is already assured of oceanic tides of deferred income through 2025 A.D.

A third ground is that of taste. The chief dignity of an artist is his art. I prefer to remember Joseph Cotten for his work in the Mercury Theater, in *Citizen Kane,* in his many fine roles, rather than for a self-conscious commercial ("I suppose you could call me a citizen of the world") for the World Savings and Loan Association. No offense meant to World—savings and loans are its business. But is it Cotten's? Henry Fonda's business is acting, not floor wax. Pat Boone's business is entertaining, not dairy products. Now and then one finds an exception like Jimmy Dean. He owns a brand of sausages, so I suppose there is some justification for his commercial, which goes, in part: "Hah. (Hi.) Ah'm Jimmy Dean. If you like a good breakfast in yore tummy, it sure would be nice if you used some of our sausage. Thank you." A modest proposal; still, I prefer his country and western songs.

I have watched once-great opera stars plugging brands of beer on TV, and I all but wept. Nobody is sacred. An old Roman of a poet, as grand as any in the books since the turn of the century, wrote paeans for the same airline which is now the inspiration for planes yet to be built. Add to poets and opera singers, a host of athletes, astronauts, dancers, comedians (Jack Benny and Bob Hope need the extra bread?), Olympic multiple gold medal winners, photographers (Ansel Adams), painters.

Which brings me to Salvador Dali. He was commissioned to turn his genius loose on the subject of the Datsun 610. He created a work entitled simply "6:10," which was reproduced in national magazine advertisements. In this painting, one of his limp, rubbery watches is deployed diagonally across a landscape of distant mountains and a vast golden plain. The hands of this watch have grown through a convenient hole in the middle of the watch. Grown is the word, because they consist of limbs of a strange tree whose roots look like horsehair. The limbs point, of course, to 6:10 on the watch. Subtle as a stick shift. Here and there about the painting, on and off the watch, are skimpy little figures—humans, horses, a dog. In the lower right quadrant of the painting is an unmounted winged horse (get it?) and a little to the southwest of this is an elaborate signature: a capitalized DALI appears in monogram design, all but enclosed within a loop under which the artist signs his *full* name. Over the signature, floating serenely, is a crown.

But the dominant feature in the painting is a spanking new red Datsun 610, resting between 9 and 12 o'clock, and photographically literal, down to the door handles and hubcaps. Sitting smack in front of his objet d'art is a lissome figure in a philosophical attitude, chin in hand, elbow on raised knee. It could be Aristotle contemplating the best of Datsun.

All credit to Datsun for commissioning a work of art. There is nothing wrong with royal, ducal, ecclesiastical, corporate or foundation commissions. Some of the pharmaceutical houses of this country have been responsible for walls full of exciting new art. But none of it, as I recall, ever enlarged an aspirin pill to function as a halo behind the head of St. Joseph, nor was there a Johnson & Johnson bandage on the knee of a naked Venus rising from a Jacuzzi.

THE INTERVIEW

AMONG THE INEXHAUSTIBLE QUARRIES OF EN-
tertainment and major appurtenances of reportage is the interview. It can do much more than exchange views, as the literal
meaning of the word suggests: It can illuminate, probe, clarify,
disabuse, becloud, denigrate, scavenge and appall, depending
on three variables: the interviewer, the interviewee and what
they discuss.

Before the day of the tape machine, the record of such exchanges relied either on the memory of the questioner, or on
the speed and accuracy of his note-taking. In Louis Biancolli's
fascinating volume, *Great Conversations,* the comments of
Wagner, Beethoven, Oscar Wilde and Walt Whitman were
drawn largely from the memory of interviewers or eavesdrop-
pers. This is no doubt why these exchanges have no rough
edges. Indeed some have an air of collaboration, as though the

reporter's style, and at times his intelligence and talents, were grafted on.

But today every last "Uh . . . er . . . you see . . . well . . . you know . . ." is faithfully reproduced. Fractured syntax, inversions, dangling participles, all the abrasions, contusions and concussions to which grammar is heir, are on display like specimens in an entomological laboratory.

I once had the ineffable honor of dining with Sandy Koufax. He is the Montesquieu of the baseball immortals, a man well read and well spoken. Not long before this meeting, I had heard him in a postgame radio interview, during which he used the all-purpose adjective "real" at least 20 times in five minutes: "I feel real good about our pennant chances"; "I threw real hard for the first six innings"; "He's a real competitor"; and so on. I said to Koufax, "You have such a good command of language, why do you pepper your interviews with all those 'reals'?" He explained that since his teammates were in the habit of listening to the interviews on a loudspeaker in the clubhouse after the game, any conspicuous departure from the patois would sound like a real pushy assertion of Koufax's articulateness; like an affront, a stroke of elitism that had no real place in the clubhouse.

In the broadcasting media, talk probably has a bigger combined audience than any other element of programming. Carson, Cavett, Griffin, Mike Douglas, Mike Wallace, Michael Jackson, Tom Snyder, Moyers, Dick Whittington, Lou Gordon, Barbara Walters—the list is endless. So is the verbiage. Clear across the mainland, and afield in Hawaii and Alaska, there are radio oracles who daily consume questions from all kinds of listeners on all manner of subjects. Some of these gurus are knowledgeable and pleasant, and dispense instant wisdom and reasonably reliable information. Others are rude, ignorant, and steeped in various shades of obnoxiousness. There are bullies who now and then humiliate an interviewee, usually over some political issue on which they disagree. The only mollifying factor in such cases is that the victim consented to be interviewed—nobody forced him at gunpoint; he should have known better. But still, even in the boxing ring, a referee will stop a contest that is badly overmatched.

Happily, most of radio's and TV's interviews and exchanges are civilized. There are old established institutions like *Meet the Press* and *Face the Nation*; nice safe interrogators like James Day on PBS; protean types like the superb Studs Terkel (himself interviewed by Day one fine night); and sound, solid Keith Berwick, who used to interview literates on KCET. That same Channel 28 properly boasted two of the best men who ever asked questions of people on camera, Charles Champlin and Art Seidenbaum; and then of course there are the redoubtable fixtures of the commercial networks, some of them bristling liberals like Edward Morgan; others perched high on the right, like William Buckley; and most of the rest settled in the broad midsection, the vast waist-land of political opinion.

But the interview has also proliferated the mighty domain of print. Most periodicals, even highly specialized ones, carry interviews. *Medical Economics,* for example, ran an 18-page section of questions it put to Ralph Nader. A fragment:

Q: Have you ever received a doctor's bill that you thought was an overcharge?

Nader: Yes.

Q: How big was the overcharge?

Nader: About twice as much as it should have been.

The *Yale Alumni Magazine,* in the course of an interview with Walker Evans, noted American photographer:

Q: Do you think it's possible for the camera to lie?

Evans: It certainly is. It almost always does.

Q: Is it all right for the camera to lie?

Evans: No, I don't think it's all right for any thing or any body to lie.

U.S. News & World Report interviewed the U.S. Commissioner of Education, Terrel H. Bell, about discipline in the schools:

Q: Are you saying that many schools were letting youngsters play around?

Bell: They surely were, and I think we're getting a welcome trend away from that. It was that laxity that caused much of the public concern and lack of public support for education.

Psychology Today has regular monthly interviews. Occasionally it brings together think-type celebrities like Robert Ardrey, author of *African Genesis,* and the late L. S. B. Leakey, anthropologist. Fragment:

Ardrey: Do you have any idea why man behaves so badly toward his fellow man? Animals don't. Why is man different from other animals?

Leakey: Lions eat zebras, but that is not aggression. That is hunting food. You are asking me about organized killing. . . . As far as I know, wild primates . . . have not reached the stage where they organize attacks on each other—for food or any other reason.

The list of interview-printing periodicals is not endless, but it is long. The nudie magazines, perhaps to persuade themselves that man does not read for skin alone, are strong for interviews. *Playboy* is especially careful to maintain an intellectual quotient to ballast the meringue, cheesecake and smut in its pages. To this end it is well served by its interviews, almost all of them of a high order. Since there are many nudie publications on the market, and aficionados of this genre are not limited to *Playboy,* it is a reasonable guess that many readers buy it for the superiority of its interviews over those in *Gallery, Penthouse, Oui* and the lesser bareskins. Although *Playboy's* interviewees are drawn from many walks (actors, athletes, economists, producers, singers, comedians), the incidence of writers is notably high: David Halberstam, Tennessee Williams, Kurt Vonnegut, Germaine Greer, Jack Anderson, Yevgeny Yevtushenko, to name only a few. *Penthouse* has interviewed William Burroughs and James Purdy; *Gallery* interviewed Truman Capote, who himself interviewed Marlon Brando for *McCall's.*

The interview form itself is by no means a modern contrivance, though its popularity and extent today are unprecedented. The dialogues of Plato take us back over 2,000 years, and there are a series of remarkable interviews in the Bible. My own favorite is that between Abraham and the Lord (Genesis 18:22–33) in which Abraham progressively persuades his creator to stay His hand against Sodom. It is a perfect model of reverse escalation of the destruction of civilians, and a lesson in humaneness to an inhumane world.

Many people object to the Niagaras of conversation that flow in electronic currents over the air, and in torrents of print on paper, but apparently more people like than dislike interviews, or else—to borrow from Lincoln—there would not be so many of them. Even criticism of verbosity has been good-natured, all things considered. Aneurin Beven, British political leader and himself a fairly garrulous talker in his time, once said of Winston Churchill:

"He never spares himself in conversation. He gives himself

so generously that hardly anyone else is permitted to give anything in his presence."

A century earlier, Sydney Smith, writer, said of Macaulay:

"He has occasional flashes of silence that make his conversation perfectly delightful."

But these comments were made by one statesman about another statesman, and by a writer about another writer, both pairs being contemporaries. That may have had something to do with it.

FANTASY IN THE ARTS

THE ARTS WITHOUT FANTASY WOULD BE LIKE an unwatered continent—topographically exciting, perhaps, but unembellished, stolid and sere. No mysterious forests, dark rivers, forbidden trees of knowledge, or man-eating plants. It might make an interesting place to visit, but I wouldn't want to live there.

One of fantasy's best friends in the arena of letters is Ray Bradbury. His short stories long ago established him as our leading missionary to the realms of the transzodiac. His stage play, *Leviathan '99*, was one of his boldest salients into outer space.

Never one to shrink from an impossible dream, Bradbury addressed himself to an almost hallucinatory premise: a captain of a spaceship, modeled upon Melville's Ahab, has been blinded by a brush with a comet named Leviathan. He cannot rest until he avenges himself by seeking out the comet and destroying it.

Now the idea of a space carrier launched from Cape Kennedy, being able to discomfit a vast astronomical object, especially one with a tail millions of miles long, is scientifically preposterous. But so is the idea of Alice shrinking, and holding converse with a caterpillar; so is the idea of a neurotic and malevolent computer which has to be gingerly defused, as in *2001*; so was that expedition by a crew, including Raquel Welch, through the veins and arteries of a living human, in *Fantastic Journey*; so are all those clearly identifiable flying objects like Mary Poppins, and Sam Small, the Flying Yorkshireman, and all the witches who ever rode aerodynamic brooms. All of them scientifically absurd.

Whatever the dramaturgical problems of *Leviathan*, Bradbury fires volley after volley of charged poetry, a series of rolling periods and arias of intense imagery, much of it powerful and beautiful. He cheerfully acknowledges a lifelong infatuation with Shakespeare and Melville; indeed the stance of his play—an attitude to which most of his critics objected—was deliberately Elizabethan/Melvillian. If *Leviathan* is not Bradbury's most successful play, it is his most daring, and we owe him something for such public acts of courage and conviction. At his best, Bradbury is magnificent; like every master of his medium, his failures are more interesting than most men's successes.

The poising of man vs. comet in *Leviathan* is obviously a mismatch. Bradbury intended that. I myself had no doubts as to who would win the showdown. On the other hand, Moby Dick, from whom Bradbury's white comet is directly descended, gave Ahab and his crew a sporting chance. Whales, after all, do get caught. (Altogether too many of them to suit the conservationists, and me.)

In comic fantasy, the fantasy of caricature, anything goes. Example: Woody Allen, as a spermatozoon in the movie, *Everything You Always Wanted to Know About Sex*. But in serious fantasy, the characters must wear a straight face and never be self-conscious. It would not do for any of Shakespeare's ghosts to be funny. They are usuely baleful, shopping for someone to avenge their murders. The ghost who moans or rattles chains is terribly old-fashioned these days; nobody writes or plays a ghost that way any longer, except to be amusing. *Topper, The Ghost and Mrs. Muir, The Ghost of Benjamin Sweet,* the ghost named O'Malley in Crockett Johnson's comic strip *Barnaby,* all represent the new generation of ghosts.

The greatest danger in fantasy is that of excess—of not knowing how far to carry a point, the danger of over-intoxication with an idea. If you stretch the imagination too far, it will snap back and refuse to perform. Once on TV there was a fantasy about an old man who had the faculty of hearing voices from the vegetable world: shrubs that whined when hungry or thirsty, and trees that cried out when cut or pruned. In a grudging way one's attention was held, which was a tribute to the program's craftsmanship, until the author could not resist the temptation to stretch his premise. He introduced some bell-shaped flowers, and these promptly gave out bell sounds. It was a greedy mixture of metaphors. Once they had us sheepishly accepting the proposition that flowers have human nervous systems, they also asked us to believe they had metal parts. That was asking too much.

There are times when too great a similitude to normal human behavior can be as ruinous as too little. In the Disney film *Lady and the Tramp*, the leading dog characters were cloying because they sounded too much like human beings in the tender moments of a soap opera. The element of caricature, which is the soul of cartoon, was destroyed. Yet in *Fantasia*, the hippos, ostriches and elephants were entirely acceptable in their grotesquerie because their choreography was dynamically wry. Tonnages and displacement and physical laws did not matter—the ballet was the thing.

The points of departure from credibility in fantasy are sometimes delicate and sometimes acute. We can believe hippos in tutus doing *Swan Lake*, but from the same factory I rejected the conceit of a whale singing opera, not because the notion was physically absurd, which it is, but because the whale was a fish (actually a mammal) out of water, and its voice was recognizably that of Nelson Eddy.

Credibility is a relative matter. We make wholesale allowances for the fantasies of children, primitives and unenlightened ancestors. We smile at and admire the hybrids of mythology, wherein a man could be half horse, and a woman half fish; wherein an Assyrian god could be part bull, part man and part eagle; wherein the Chimera had a lion's head, a goat's body, a serpent's tail, and breathed fire; wherein Leda coolly miscegenated with a swan. But science has come a long way, and we no longer hybridize species so rakishly. Linnaeus and Darwin were of great help there.

Whole religions are based on elements of fantasy, almost always couched in terms of parable and drama. Our own story of the Creation, and various versions invented by the Aztecs, Polynesians, Eskimos and Greeks—each has its own splendid mythology. We are brought upon the serpent in the garden, the flaming bush, the talking ass, the regurgitating whale, the lions of Daniel, instant healing and other familiar miracles.

We have a rich demonology, too—and a good thing. For without the opposite side of the canvas from the sublime religious art of Da Vinci, Michelangelo, Raphael and a host of others, we should not have the prodigies of Hieronymous Bosch, Parentino, Traini, the eschatological paintings of El Greco and Goya, and kindred masters of the grisly.

In our own time, of course, fantasy springs from more familiar sources—our waking and sleeping dreams. It is always open season for surrealism: Klee, Dali, Escher and Ernst are right up there in the ratings with Freud and Jung. Movies and TV have moved with increasing boldness into the light and heavy fantastic—pictures like *8½, Kwaidan, Images, The Journey, Planet of the Apes, War of the Worlds, The Discreet Charm of the Bourgeoisie*; sequences like the nightmare ballet in *Fiddler on the Roof*; television series like *Twilight Zone, Star Trek, Outer Limits*.

Well, that's fine. Keep them coming. Keep the dream factories working overtime. The imagination needs regular exercise in this prosaic world of stock market reports, body counts, traffic bulletins, tax laws, yellow pages and questionnaires. If the arts don't give us fantasy, the city council and the chamber of commerce never will.

BOSTON

THE LOGO OF STATION WHDH, MASSACHU-
setts anchor of public television, carries in big letters the name
of BOSTON, which comes up from somewhere just short of
infinity until it fills the tube and rushes past you, going
through your room and on into outer space, no doubt to orbit
forever around the sun.

And every time this happens I think of the city where I was
born and grew up, where I matriculated as a fan of the once
Boston Braves and the ongoing Red Sox, Celtics and Bruins;
and where I acquired what is alleged to be a Bostonian accent.

From where I sit in front of a TV set, I have not yet seen
what I would be willing to accept as a definitive program on
Boston. Neither bicentennial nor any other kind of program.
There have been some pretty good attempts, but somehow
none has seemed to get at, or into, the *anima* of the city.
Beacon Hill, a commercial network casualty after a brief ex-

posure to the perils of the wasteland, was set in Boston, but it could have been about people in New Haven or Oxnard, for all the resonances it twanged in me. But then perhaps I would be impossible to satisfy; and this acknowledgment brings me face to face with a theory; to wit, that no stranger can properly grasp an elbow, let alone the soul of a city. Many films are shot in cities, but mostly the function of the *urbs* is that of background; it becomes in a sense moving wallpaper. But when filmmakers have been marinated in cities and country-side, and know them viscerally, then these places become presences, characters, members of the cast. Thus the Rome and the *villaggios* of Fellini, Rossellini, de Sica; the Indian hamlets of Satayajit Ray, the *campagne* of Renoir, Buñuel's Spain, Bergman's Sweden, the Manhattan of Lumet.

Yes, there have been movies shot in Boston. *Love Story, Charlie* and *The Boston Strangler,* to name three. But as in *Beacon Hill,* the city in these productions was mainly diorama with sound, and not integral to the people and the action. To explain better what I mean about the inwardness of growing up in a place, I beg indulgence for a clump of reminiscences, some shading toward irrelevance, about Boston and its harbor and a certain purlieu named for the first governor of Massachusetts Bay Colony. They relate not to the Boston of J. P. Marquand, nor the city of the Cabots, Lodges and Lowells, but to freight yards, street grids and the waters of the bay.

From a third-floor tenement on Bremen Street in East Boston, one could look out across a railroad freight-switching complex and beyond the vapors of the city dump to the middle reaches of Boston Harbor; and there was Governor's Island—gone now, swallowed up by Logan International Airport—and the long trestle of the Boston, Revere Beach & Lynn Railroad, also gone; and Wood Island, a recreational area, still there.

It was Italian and Jewish where we lived, and some Irish, and they mixed indifferently well. The streets were named for men and places and battles, the long streets after the far cities—Bremen, Chelsea, Havre (not *Le* Havre), London, Paris; the short ones after American military men of medium renown: Marion, Putnam, Prescott, Brooks; and somebody in the city council had remembered the poets, for there were streets farther east, toward Orient Heights, named Byron, Shelley, Wordsworth, Moore and Keats. And the Revolution, which had primed itself in these parts (the Tea Party at a wharf just across the way, Bunker Hill not as far in another direction), was nicely integrated in the lattice of the street plan: the trolley cars to Bowdoin Square rolled along Bennington Street, which was parallel to Saratoga and Eutaw and Trenton and Ticonderoga.

And if you love America, it is good to have the epitaphs of its history mixed up in your childhood, in the serum of your nostalgia. The James Otis Primary School. And the Ulysses S. Grant Grammar School. And Miss Emma Bates Harvey, sister of the governor of the state, a great, heavy woman who was my teacher and had been my mother's teacher too, and who smiled on me and my betters like a Yankee She-Buddha. She was calm and wise and stately, and just about the closest I ever came to the dignity that must have been old Massachusetts, the Athenian state of Emerson and Longfellow and Whittier and Melville and men's men of that kind, who are no more.

The economic mean of the neighborhood was a chronic struggle to stay solvent, and this status was accepted without complaint or bitterness. If other people in other parts lived better, why good for them. We no more measured ourselves against them than we did against the people of Borneo who at that time occasionally ate each other.

When I was still a kid, the family removed to Winthrop, first of the shore towns north of Boston but so close, as a sea gull flies, that Yaz on a good day could throw out a base runner on Runway 2 at Logan. We lived almost in the shadow of a first-class drumlin called Winthrop Head, one lot removed from the shore drive that abutted on the Atlantic. Left behind were the freight yards. No longer the cough and chug of shunting engines and the clash of couplings. On summer nights as I lay in bed in the attic room with a dormer window, I would listen to water lapping against the sea wall—a susurrant stirring, lazy and remote, but interrupted now and then by a sudden hard slap as though to remind the brooding shore who was boss. Under a full moon, and at spring tide, the sea needed no winds from beyond the horizon to show muscle. Waves struck the wall before they even began to curl, and the shock made houses in our sector shudder as though from a temblor.

In winter, under the stress of a nor'easter, combers charged and battered the wall. Seams of cement binding huge granite blocks were gutted and washed out; as the tide rose, so did the waves. Out of a frothing explosion of water, a two-ton slab would be catapulted across the drive to land on someone's lawn, like an instant monument. The sea poured through the breach, ripped out clay and gravel from the roadbed, carved up chunks of macadamized pavement, and made off with the whole mess like a mad vandal. By the time the tide backed down, there would be gaping caves two city blocks long in the side of Shore Drive.

The inevitable big storm of the season brought newsreel cameramen and sightseers from Boston, only 15 minutes away;

repair crews followed. Craters were filled, the pavement
sealed, and vulnerable joints in the wall fortified by bulwarks
of riprap; but the following winter it would all be torn down
again. In despair the state ultimately rewrote the configuration
of the shoreline. Breakwaters and jetties were laid down,
uglifying what had been a graceful crescent between two
drumlins, until today the shore is no longer nakedly exposed
to the Atlantic, with Spain the next landfall; now it is con-
fronted by offshore bastions of gray riprap streaked with bird
droppings and pocked with barnacles.

The window of my attic room faced due east, and so did my
pillow. Any time I opened my eyes at night, there was Graves
Light five miles out, sweeping in short flashes, resting, then
flashing again, its beam powerful enough to play on the wall
behind me. And if I got up and went to the window and
looked out to the southeast, there was Boston Light, its bright
steady eye waxing and waning in unhurried rotation, appropriate to its rank of the oldest lighthouse in America (first
lighted in 1716).

I never curtained that window. The rising sun was my
alarm clock. Every degree in the chromatic scale of dawn—
red, gray, roseate, dappled, golden, alert orange, precaution
blue, atomic purple, starred by the planet Mercury, barred by
strands of cloud, nebulous with zodiacal light, all appeared in
the frame. Most of the time in clear weather I was aroused by
the dazzle of the sun's rim as it first edged over the horizon.
Now and then I would get up before the rest of the house—
even before my father, who into his 100th year arose daily at
5 A.M.—and I would walk along the beach. The work of night
waters had smoothed the strand's only stretch of sand and
erased every print of man, dog, gull and crab. In those lambent

dawn moments I felt deliciously alone, like an Adam on the shore of creation, not yet suspecting the idea of a snake.

Winthrop's shore takes a side view of outer Boston Harbor and its many islands, the gift of glaciers immemorial. No other American harbor is so brimming with history and romance, nor as rich in blunt, coarse names—an unfastidious mixture of menagerie, larder and hard times; Hog Island, Snake Island, The Roaring Bulls, Calf Island, Deer Island, Ram's Head Bar, Raccoon Island, Pig Rock, Cat Island, Bug Light, Apple Island, Grape Island, Nut Island, Egg Rock Light, Thimble Island, Bumpkin Island, Ragged Island, Shag Rocks, Shirley Gut, the Misery Islands, Hangman's Island, Sailor's Island, Nix's Mate, Spectacle Island, World's End, Moon Island. With names like those, what does a city need of Saltonstalls and Ticknors?

But this has been only about names, streets, teachers, storms, lighthouses and islands. All of the above is just a morsel of one native's sense of a city's ambience. It would take many more pages than are at our disposal to begin to approach the essence of what has happened to downtown Boston, and its Back Bay, and its west side. And brood over what has happened to South Boston.

But be all this as it may, I will continue to watch the zooming logo of WHDH, in the hope that one of these nights it will be followed by a miracle on the tube, in which a truly dimensional Boston will be there in living color. I have waited long, and am prepared to wait longer.

THE DOCUDRAMA-
TELEMENTARY

WHENEVER A VAST OCCASION COMES ALONG—
the death of a president, the visit of a pope, a round trip to
the moon, an East-West detente garnished with honor guards,
a national election, the Watergate hearings—then the same
medium which brings us so many hours of whodunits, private
eyes, game shows, old movies, reruns, trivia and recycled slop
becomes vital, dynamic, resourceful, imaginative and sporadi-
cally magnificent. These finest hours are all documentary.
They are not called such, but that is what they are.

It happens that TV and the documentary have a special
affinity. Whereas the big eye has crippled or destroyed whole
entities like radio drama, periodicals (*Look, Life, Collier's*),
B-pictures, newspapers and living room conversation, and has
affected God knows what else that is not measurable by any
economic index, at the same time it has been the documentary's best friend.

194

Before television, the documentary film had been, relatively speaking, an esoteric branch of an otherwise popular medium. One proof of the rare-bird nature of the early documentary is to ask yourself how many of the following names you recognize: Anstey, Cavalcanti, Flaherty, Grierson, Ivens, Leacock, Legg, Lorentz, Rotha, Ruttman, Strand, Wright. Beyond Grierson and Flaherty, who are at least known to students of film, the rest mean nothing to most of us. Yet every one was important to the history of the documentary.

It was not our fault that these people were not part of our experience, as were Griffith, Chaplin, De Mille, Lubitsch and a hundred other film familiars that we grew up on. The fault, if it can be called a fault, lay in the disinterest of motion picture exhibitors; there was no chance for documentaries to get a big audience so long as audiences were not exposed to them in any form. And without big audiences, there was no big money to produce them; and so the cycle was closed.

A generation ago, the term documentary was seldom heard. Movie people and exhibitors referred to documentaries by length, not character; they were "shorts." Just shorts. If a feature-length documentary was made, they didn't know what to call it, and worse, they didn't know where to put it. Mostly they just ignored it, and let it die.

But TV soon discovered that the documentary was not a luxury, not a freak, not an arty vehicle, but a necessity. Because the medium is immediate, simultaneous and widespread, it shares certain characteristics with newspapers and radio— the need, indeed the compulsion, to gather and disseminate news, and to deal with information and public opinion as vital commodities.

The term "documentary" itself has ceased to frighten people. For a while the television industry searched desperately for a viable synonym, to get away from the fancied or actual stigma of the term. They came up with "telementaries," "docu-dramas" and "fact-dramas." All uniformly starchy and self-conscious names, all happily stillborn.

The news documentary came naturally to TV; the theme documentary followed after a while, and quickly became sophisticated. Basic reportage was outlined with skills that had not been considered necessary or important to factual content: music, planned photography (as against candid or sponta-neous), carefully structured writing. The documentary began to make larger statements, as in the case of Edward R. Mur-row's disposal of Senator Joseph McCarthy, the controversial *The Selling of the Pentagon, Point of Order, Titicut Follies,* the barrage of films on our unhappy adventure in Vietnam, ringing tocsins on ecology, prison reform, the population explo-sion, our shrinking resources, and so on into the awards season.

A measure of the effectiveness of documentaries on political or social subjects, especially when they concerned military, economic or administrative issues, was the uproar they created. Instead of being damned with faint praise, they were praised with loud damns. Denials, assertions, accusations, angry charges, subpoenas. Whether or not these pictures cast much light, they generated a good deal of heat. To their credit, let it be said; for a supine medium, stereotyped forms, a play-it-safe attitude and an unbalanced diet of medics, spies, cowboys, sitcoms and giveaways, is of small value to the public, the country, or our time. Even as entertainment, a tenth rerun of *Hogan's Heroes* or *I Love Lucy* would appear to stand on the threshold of diminishing returns.

As archive, the documentary flourished. Television opened vaults that seemed as sealed as Tut's tomb. Old series like

Victory at Sea, The Churchill Years, The FDR Series, would run for 26 weeks, sometimes longer. To feed them, research teams scoured private and government film libraries, and turned up what in film was the equivalent of ancient scrolls, artifacts, potsherds and gemstones. It is conceivable that the film depositories will be all mined out some day, like coral reserves, but there is no sign of that being imminent. New series, like Bronowski's *Ascent of Man* keep coming along, and manage to satisfy the standards of both good documentary-making and good history. Esthetic trips like Sir Kenneth Clark's *Civilization* series put in a good word for the abiding values of culture; excursions into recent history (*The Rise and Fall of the Third Reich, Wattstax, Visions of Eight*) are vivid chronicles that should endure on the permanent shelf.

The compilation documentary is not necessarily sober, relevant, foreboding or rhetorical. An Academy nomination, *Legendary Heroes,* had to do with heavyweight boxing champions of the past. It has incredible footage, some of which must have been found in attics and rummage sales from Finland to Australia. Every so often somebody puts together an anthology of comedy scenes, or dance numbers, or great moments in football or aviation. This is mostly scissors-and-cement stuff, but even at its least imaginative it is instructive, like an illustrated article in an encyclopedia, or a book on succulents.

The creative documentary grows in all directions. If you like animals, there are Irwin Rosten's fine works on the grizzly bear and the maligned wolf, Paul Radin's classic reenactment, *Born Free* (lions), and dozens of pictures on apes, penguins, white sharks, even one on a rare snail. If you like the taste of salt, there are the Cousteau specials and Bruno Vailati's *The Seven Seas.* If you are concerned with being overweight, then you must—repeat, must—see *A Matter of Fat,* produced with its usual fine hand by the National Film Board of Canada. If only you can find the picture in a theater, that is.

We are accustomed to great changes taking place periodically in stage and film drama, and these changes are marked off by such familiar terms as neo-realist, avant garde, new wave, theater of the absurd. The changes in the documentary film have been as many if not more, but they are not as well known or codified, because until recently the documentary itself was not well known. That has been altered, thanks largely to the tube, not the movie houses. For where, in any big city, on any weekend, can a man take his children, his Ms., or just himself, to see a picture that comments directly, informationally, factually, upon the world around us, be it a film on volcanoes or whales or obesity or Jack Johnson or autistic children or Beethoven or Soutine or future shock? Not many outlets. Maybe an art house or two.

Fortunately, though, one can stay at home and see grizzlies and sharks and old-time heavyweights at odd hours. Whatever TV's sins, and they are many, it did bring the documentary in from Siberia and gave it a warm home just across the tracks from the mansions of Lucy, Hogan, Gilligan, Welby and M. Tyler Moore. Be grateful for big-sized favors.

C & C

AMONG FAMILIAR ABBREVIATIONS OF PROCE-
dures affecting health and bodily function are EKG, IUD
and D & C, the last two known especially to women. I now
propose a procedure to be known as C & C, which would
relate to the health of the body politic, and to the function of
media.

C & C stands for Conscience and Communications. We
would have little trouble agreeing on what we mean by communications, but conscience is another matter. It tends to vary
from age to age, country to country, and man to man. It was
considered perfectly conscionable at one time to enslave whole
peoples, but this is no longer tolerable in peace treaties. In fact
we are now very kind to vanquished nations. We pet them,
we release their war criminals, along with our own, and we
send them lakes of Coca-Cola.

The conscience of Vatican City is not to be confused with

that of Las Vegas; Sitting Bull's conscience was not Custer's; the conscience of the Kremlin is not Jerusalem's. What distinguishes one from the other is not simply right or wrong, good or bad, but a whole plexus of traditions, convictions, objectives and interests.

So it is with American conscience. It is not one thing but many. The conscience of the sheep and the wolf, of Jefferson and of Madison Avenue, of the Supreme Court and South Boston, of William Buckley and Daniel Ellsberg. There is also the conscience of the mass, and the conscience of mass media.

Whenever there is a revolution today, among the first tangibles seized by the rebels are the radio and TV stations, and the newspapers. It follows that if a transmitter is attractive to the enemies of an established order, it must also be attractive to the friends. For transmitters and presses are not only mechanisms but vehicles—carriers of whatever content is poured into them. They are purveyors of the Word, the ideology, the big or little truth, the big or little lie, credulity, or the gaps in it; the mirror that reflects a culture, as well as the mold that stamps its form.

In a stable and quiet society, radio and TV are mild and benign, pursuing an even tenor, as in the Scandinavian countries, or, let's say, New Zealand. In a monolithic society, as in the Soviet Union, they are humble and obedient servants of the state; in a country controlled by a powerful state religion, as in most of Islam, they are a sort of super minaret, from which the muezzins of government call the faithful to periodic war.

But I address myself to the nature of communications in this country, for in many ways we are unique. We are bigger, richer, more sophisticated, and certainly more competitive than most. After all, it was we who developed the singing commercial, the double feature, the oracle who takes calls on radio, the Western, the giveaway program, the celebrity salesman and the child huckster.

Now there are many ways of defining communications. My own candidate is one that has stood the test of two centuries —a definition proposed by John Adams in his correspondence with Thomas Jefferson. He spoke of the proprietors of the press as being without doubt the most powerful aristocracy ever created by a democracy. And he went on to spell out an aristocrat as "anyone who influences as much as a single other person, by the persuasion of his fortune, eloquence, science, learning, craft or cunning."

If radio and TV had existed in his time, John Adams would certainly have included them among his aristocracy, for they are extraordinary persuaders. TV especially has the power to arouse or anesthetize social conscience. It has the awesomely momentous capacity to sway elections. It can be more effective on occasion, than the machinery of government itself, as was shown in the McCarthy, Watergate and impeachment committee telecasts. These hearings were in themselves inconclusive, but the long, close, candid look at the principals permitted the public to draw its own conclusions, and decide the next elections.

If, as historians claim, it was the father image of Eisenhower over the professional brother-in-law image of Adlai Stevenson; if it was Pierre Salinger's unsettling jowls and Ronald Reagan's B-picture beauty that defeated one and elected the other, then TV must be granted the respect that we give to the most effective weapons and instruments. The more powerful the hardware, the more caution about using it—the ultimate symbol of this equation being the H-bomb. We are not nearly as nervous and watchful as we should be over the uses to which we put the weaponry and hardware of media, which directly affect education and general culture.

It is only fair to say that American networks have done, from time to time, and are constantly capable of doing superior and conscionable work. So that when I make a charge of willful downgrading in the overall picture, I do so in full awareness that there do exist archipelagos of excellence, whose member islands appear, disappear and reappear like those un- decided volcanic extrusions of the South Pacific. But alas, American broadcasting has too often inflicted on its audience a mediocrity unparalleled in the long and complicated annals of communications. I believe the process has not been acci- dental. Indeed the deliberateness of it could be its biggest sin.

If a low mean were the result of insufficient talent or funds, or lack of know-how, or honest miscalculation, it would be easier to accept. But mediocrity is a business. It is the knowing partner of conformity; as it goes up, cultural levels come down. The late Alexander King once had a TV program of his own; he had not been doing it for very long when he got a memo- randum of pained complaint from his producer: "I don't mind your having 20 percent intellectual stuff on the show, but last week 50 percent of it called for the audience to have a high school education." Mediocrity is an industry, like making low- quality shirts for low-income consumers at a low price, or shooting witless catastrophe movies for audiences that have not had their fill of catastrophes, like two world wars and a dozen lesser ones.

Our broadcasters have succeeded in conditioning a people once accustomed to seeing a play or a film without interrup- tion, to tolerate the fragmentizing of movies by as many as 20 to 40 commercials. We can hardly hear a weather report or news bulletin save through the courtesy of a sponsor; we are caught between the hard sell and the soft sell, in everything from deodorants and cushy-cushy products, to rationalizations for price-gouging and double-dipping.

A teacher once asked a student whether, if he could get away with it, he would steal $10,000. "Sure," replied the boy, "It would be OK so long as I kept busy and didn't have time to think about what I had done." In other words, it would be OK so long as his conscience were given no time to assert itself. Now while our mass media are not stealing units of $10,000, they are too often robbing the public of something much more valuable, something irreplaceable—and that is time. Time in which to do what Walter Lippmann warned us to be about: "If we don't harden ourselves by stretching ourselves upward to not wholly attainable ideals, we slump down into flabbiness and footlessness and boredom." And what more could any deadly enemy wish for us in this nuclear age? Are American communications, in the words of that boy, too busy to think about what they are doing? Too busy paying dividends? So busy the conscience cannot operate? But the question also occurs, whether the 200-plus millions of citizens are themselves too busy to worry about conscience.

"After the first blush of sin," wrote Thoreau, "comes indifference to it, and from immoral it becomes unmoral, and not quite unnecessary to the life that we have made."

I am afraid that the sins of our mass media are being received with the indifference of which Thoreau spoke. The audience does not seem to care that much. The issue finally boils down to whether the media have any conscience worthy of the name; and if they do have, how much of it is exercised; and if it is not exercised, why not?

If the panels of artistic communication are in the hands of

timid or venal men; if mediocrity and a low mean are contrived because they are profitable and convenient; if monster
and nude movies are to be seen every night of the week in key
cities, while serious and well-made films struggle for a play
date; if rock groups, for all their genuine brilliance, roll in
Rollses while the symphony orchestras and chamber groups of
the land beg abjectly for support, then something is wrong
at the base of the pyramid, and not only at the top.

I call upon still one more friendly witness, old man Plato,
who said, "What is honored in a country will be cultivated
there." The task is clear: to cultivate that which is worthy,
and then to honor it. Education can help, but it is the duty of
mass communications, which are the most powerful educators
of all, to lead more than to follow; to mold higher tastes, and
not pander to the lowest.

As a rich country, an *in* country, we can afford to make our
culture safer for the conscionable artist and the conscionable
audience. After all, we are not a dowdy republic, or a bedlam
of 40 political parties, or a maelstrom of a hundred fanatic
religions. Being awake, we have need to sing, and not just
commercials. We are entitled to have poets as well as bunny
clubs; to give time on the screen and TV to muses as well as
to monsters. We have an obligation to ourselves and our
posterity, to hitch our wagons to stars, as well as blast off space
probes to Jupiter.

THE PURSUIT OF THE
PURSUIT OF HAPPINESS

"THE PURSUIT OF HAPPINESS" IS A FELITICIOUS phrase in all seasons, but it has a much different meaning today from what it meant when it was drafted by Thomas Jefferson 200 years ago, into the preamble to the American Declaration of Independence. A common assumption is that revolutionists are firebrands, aggressively on the move, and shrill; but Jefferson was soft-spoken, gentle and contemplative, he admired the quiet philosophers, and in his maturity he could write to his friend James Madison, "Agreeable society is the first essential in constituting the happiness and of course the value of our existence."

That was Jefferson in his forties. In his thirties, at the time he wrote the phrase that has become as famous as any four consecutive words in any language, happiness had a far more exalted and universal denotation; it meant freedom from tyranny and unjust taxation, the option of working profitably, the enjoyment of basic rights, and a chance to live life as one saw fit.

Definitions of happiness have never been in short supply, both before and after Jefferson, and the means to achieve happiness have never lacked advocates. Virtue and truth, said Coleridge, are the only way to happiness; union with God, said Pascal; sharing, said Byron; being loved, said Victor Hugo; consistency in living, said Goethe; have either a clear conscience or none at all, suggested Ogden Nash; make others happy, said Ingersoll; suffering helps, recommended Plutarch; make yourself busy with the unimportant, said Edward Newton; touch a hundred flowers but pick none, wrote Alice Duer Miller.

It all comes down to taste, as La Rochefoucauld recognized before Jefferson was born. "Happiness is dependent on the taste, and not on things," he said. "It is by having what we like that we are made happy, not having what others think desirable." But what we like is conditioned by culture, religion, environment, education, experience, and especially by our mental and physical health. And yet we are creatures of personal taste only up to a permissible point: society takes over, more and more, by invading the private precincts of character and relationships, like a greedy weed rampant in a garden. For what does it avail a man who has achieved the prerequisites to happiness, if he must surrender them all to go off and fight in a distant war for a dubious objective? A man may have arrived at the tranquility of Buddha, but if his meditations are choked by smog, or disrupted by the screaming of jet engines because his retreat is on the approach to an airport, then he may have a little trouble staying on pitch.

The difference between the pursuit of happiness in Jefferson's time and in ours, is that it was then measured, and had dignity; today it is frantic. Happiness has never been more relentlessly pursued than it is now: why is all that vast Amazon of alcohol pouring through the world? And the tons of marijuana and heroin and cocaine and opium and LSD, being processed, sold, consumed? On what does astrology batten? Everywhere in America are "personal encounter" groups, in which people seek happiness through contact and communication. "Therapy"—group and individual—is no longer a clinical term, but is bandied about in living rooms. What is the staggering divorce rate, but a struggle with boa constrictors of unhappiness?

Happiness has become synonymous with anodyne. Television is largely electronic nepenthe. The glory holes of Las Vegas, Reno, Monte Carlo, the tens of thousands of crowded night clubs, bars, discotheques, the multitudinous open-air rock sessions, all offer the cosmic drugs of stimulation, submersion, and escape from reality. The search for the nipple of happiness has become desperate, and for its grimness we have mainly three institutions to thank: politics, for its lust for power, its passion to control human and material resources even at the cost of war; industry, for its ruthless pollution of man's diminishing natural environment; and organized religion for its stubborn indifference to the hard menace that mankind may well die from too much of itself.

It is therefore heartening, in the midst of growing worldwide anxiety and unhappiness, to find there is also a growing concern, and that people are stirring themselves to do something about it. Many people—not enough by any means—but still a respectable number, are raising their voices and raising funds. One of these voices was an organization based in Japan, called PHP, for "Peace and Happiness Through Prosperity." Its prospectus was quick to explain that by prosperity it didn't mean easy living, but moral and spiritual richness achieved through individual initiative and conscience. It published a digest type of magazine whose texts, drawn from writers in 50 countries, were addressed to "understanding the rules for living" that will enable us to find the happiness we all seek. "Man," it concluded, "must be the starting point of our research." This objective aligned PHP with a distinguished company including Alexander Pope, in whose best known essay is the advice that the proper study of mankind is man. That prescription is 250 years old, but it is still good.

The pursuit continues.

FRAGGING
AND BRAGGING

TELEVISION IS NOT THE ONLY MEDIUM WHOSE commercials can be a fragging nag. (Frag: *v.t.*, from frag- mentize, to blow up an officer with a grenade, as was done occasionally by disgruntled personnel in Vietnam; also, to bombard a program with anywhere from 14 to 48 commercials, as is done often on the longer shows, and always on the late talkfests.) Yes, it can be said that videoblurbs are not the only ads that try the patience and philosophy of the con- sumer; they are only the most conspicuous, widespread and frequent.

At times one yearns for the quiet boasting of commercials that existed long before broadcasting—the ads in printed media. I recently studied a few, selecting only those in an organ of undisputed quality and substance. What better choice than *The New Yorker*? I went through some issues at random, and came to the conclusion that in advertising, just as in the world which staggers all around us, there is no safe place. While there are none of the unsavory, irritating or wearying messages that come to us with the speed of light in broadcasting, and while one always has the option of skipping ads entirely (something not easily done in TV or radio because of the time factor—you must wait for the commercial to be over), nevertheless even in slick periodicals, the advertising is occasionally gross, vulgar or kitsch. On a higher level than TV, to be sure, but still impeachable.

For example, because readers of *The New Yorker* tend to be trim of heel, the very expensiveness of a product is sometimes starred. "Just think," a full-page color ad bids us muse, "for the price of a Rolls Royce you can own a good watch." It then goes on to expand on the glories of the Audemars Piguet Grande Complication timepiece, billed as "the costliest watch in the world," and priced at $25,000. "If you want one," you are cautioned, "you'll have to wait two years." Then comes a note of reassurance which will make life brighter for those of us who cannot afford the model: "Of course, there are Audemars Piguets that are somewhat more available, at the prices of Ferraris, Mercedes, Cadillacs, and even Fiats."

There is something about the French. Boissiere is commended to us "because the best gin deserves the most expensive vermouth." Eau de Joy of Jean Patou declares itself "the costliest perfume in the world." Cordon Rouge does not claim to be the most expensive brew of its kind, simply "the finest champagne the world has ever known." Bisquit Cognac is "the noblest Napoleon of them all."

World supremacy is announced by all kinds of herrenvolk products. Under a photograph of the earth as seen from the moon, runs the legend, "One world. One piano. Steinway & Sons." Revere Ware is "the world's most glamorous cook and serveware"; Metaxa is "the world's most awarded after-dinner drink"; Blackglama is "the world's finest natural dark ranch mink"; Bushmills is "the world's oldest whiskey"; Crown Royal is "the world's finest Canadian whiskey"; Rodell makes "the world's most advanced electronic pocket calculator"; Jarlsberg Cheese tells us that "In Norway . . . you'll find the richest milk in the world"; according to the Bahama Islands Tourists Office, "the waters of the Bahamas are more beautiful than anywhere else in the world" (maybe grammar and syntax are not required courses in Bahaman schools); Universal Genève makes "the thinnest shock resistant automatic watches in the world"; Chanel 19 is "the world's most famous bottle"; the Franklin Mint is "the world's foremost private mint." Only once did I find a moment's hesitation in a claim of world supremacy, and that was in an ad of the Regency Hotel: "The most civilized hotel in New York. Maybe the world."

Other products boldly move in on life itself, and profess intimacy with, and even involvement in, our fortunes. I have seen nothing so stunning in print as TV's ecstatic cry, "He touched me! He touched me!" alluding to the fact that an unidentified and unseen male touched a lady deponent by or with Chantilly, after which, we are told, "suddenly nothing is the same!" But there is on paper, much less hysterical though still fervid, the inspiriting assurance that "No one wants the evening to end when there's friendship, good conversation and Cointreau."

Nubile girls and/or women are urged to "Be Somebody" by wearing a Formfit Rogers bra. The only possible inference is that without this support, a female runs the hazard of being nobody. Countess Mara, her ads say, designs for "one man in a million." That would seem rather uneconomical, since on the basis of the adult male population of the United States, the

countess, at this rate, would not have more than 80 or 90 customers across the country. Then we learn that success is
measurable by the rum you drink: "When you make it with
Myers's, you've made it. It's a rum that means you've come
up in the world." Not to be upstaged by rum, a brand of gin
takes cognizance of the need of man, in this fragging existence
of ours, to make a right choice somewhere along the line. We
are told "It's worth the price to have at least one thing in your
life that's absolutely perfect. Tanqueray Gin."

Loew's Drake Hotel in New York City is proud of its "great
restoration of the good things in life," and refers to itself as
"a splendid hotel on a marvelous corner of Park Avenue . . .
where everything's coming up roses and crystal and gilt."

Both printed and broadcast advertisements can get real
philosophic like. A luxury industry ran an ad which endorses
amour propre and self-expression: "How to say, 'I love me'
. . . It's right to tell the world how you feel. About ideas.
About emotions. About you." It then revs up to a pitch for
pelts by the American Fur Industry.

An anodyne to our woes is suggested by the makers of a
pewter figure of a boy standing with hands behind his back,
blowing a balloon of bubble gum. "Troubles go pop," says the
text, "at the sight of this carefree little lad." Not *my* troubles.
They don't pop easily, and never at the sight of gum being
chewed, whether by a light-foot lad in pewter, or by baseball
manager Dick Williams, kneading Doublemint at 1,175 rpm
through an entire ball game.

If Formfit Rogers should not quite succeed in making a girl
feel like Somebody, there are other resorts, like the Queen
Victoria Apron. Its ad takes us back into history: "Queen
Victoria Would Have Loved It! . . . An old-fashioned hostess
apron is what Queen Victoria might have worn for a dinner *à*

deux with darling Albert . . . Look (and feel) like a queen: order your Queen Victoria apron today." (Parentheses and italics are Queen Victoria's.)

Now if all this documentation makes you reach for something to settle your stomach, then hold! There are *modest* ads, and good ones too. Bang & Olufsen advertise "fine instruments for the reproduction of music." A condominium in Longboat Key, Florida, invites you to "stay at a quiet place." Yousuf Karsh, photographer, simply announces his availability for portraits by appointment. The Madison Hotel of Washington, D.C., avers it is "elegant, quiet, unruffled—never a convention," and then almost spoils it by adding the snob touch, "Washington's Correct Address." A line of pottery whose name I regret having forgotten, describes itself as "calculated to please." Baldwin Piano pictures a section of a keyboard, under which it says only, "Erroll Garner's Accompanist." A brand of lamps makes a little joke, "Is Tatu Too Too For You?"

The two ads that I remember most warmly down the years were modest ones. In a New Hampshire town one day I saw a billboard for a kitchen range which read, "Bardes Ranges Are Very Good." And in a London subway during the war, there was a sign on the back of a seat, reading, "No Smoking In This Car. Not Even Abdullahs."

As for those products which seek to persuade, and the buyers who are influenced by the dazzle of something being the most expensive of its kind, I have only this comment: At one time, Vincent van Gogh was the least expensive painter in the world. Even then, he sold only one painting. It went for 50 francs. And who do you suppose bought it? Another painter.

PIFFLE

FOR THE FIRST TIME SINCE THE PRIMAL CON-
cept of entertainment was worked up into a public performance by enterprising bushmen, piffle now enjoys a regular
mass audience. Protracted palaver that would not be tolerated
in a theater, or in print, fills hour upon hour of radio and
television, and enough people listen and watch to make it
highly profitable.

Hosts and guests (a sorry stretch of those once convivial
terms) gather in studios and exchange compliments, anecdotes, trivial information and naked plugs, interrupted only by
frequent "messages" (another semantic comedown) from
multiple sponsors, and by pauses for station identification
which are far more than pauses: usually five seconds of identification, and closer to five minutes of clustered commercials.

Gab itself can be amusing and may even be artful, as im-
plied in the gently approving idiom, "the gift of gab." There

have been some masters of this skill on the air, like the late Alex King and the early (before he left TV) Woody Allen. But most of those who gather around hot mikes and cameras are specialists in charisma more than masters of discussion.

There is something about the format of these events which induces inanity, like the Academy Awards presentations that never fail to generate embarrassing moments. In the latter, someone thanks too many people too profusely, or spatters everybody with an ammoniacal ego, or reminds you of how many Oscars he-she has won before this one, or stuns you with a hammerstroke of bad taste.

Several factors contribute to this. One is the occasion itself: people from many walks—singers, acrobats, authors, couturiers, returned astronauts, vice-presidents who resign under indictment, headline-makers of all sorts (or, in the case of award presentations, actors whose lines have always been written for them, sound men who have never uttered a sound in public, directors who have directed everybody but themselves, etc.)—all these diverse types come together in unrehearsed, uncontrolled situations. People who even in their private lives don't know what to say when they are praised or receive a gift, suddenly find themselves having to acknowledge an award before a large audience. Some of them become self-conscious; they strain to be witty or modest or gracious or profound, and if they do not come by these attributes naturally, the effect is usually awkward.

Then again there is the sheer size of the canvas—the time to be consumed. Guests who have a lot to say and little time in which to say it, manage, if they are at all nimble, to be succinct. But if there is time to kill, they drift into conversational sprawl, and the substance fritters away.

The role of host is not easy. Not everyone is a bottomless

mine of knowledge or a font of charm, and when a shallow host interacts with shallow guests, the resulting piffle proliferates like hungry bacilli in a heaven of agar-agar.

Virtuosos in fields other than conversation do not necessarily make good hosts. Sammy Davis, Jr., for example—a superb entertainer of song and dance, but no great jawsmith on his own TV show. Sometimes it was hard for me to follow his discourses because I was so dazzled by the jewelry that flashed from his fingers and wrists, and no sooner did I succeed in overlooking them, than I was numbed by his effusiveness in admiring—over-admiring—some pale witticism by a guest. He would roll his head in laughter, slap his (or his guest's) knee, pronounce the joke and its author *terrific*, and prattle on like an adolescent at a beach party after drinking two beers.

The lovely and talented Dinah Shore, as TV hostess, was a model of stately blandness. Merv Griffin was the medium's most successful transmogrification of tapioca. Feisty hosts aroused more interest because there was bound to be controversy on their programs, but one eventually tired of their constant ax-grinding. Jack Paar in his heyday was better at the practice of personality than of conversation: Dick Cavett was skilled in both, and one of the best of the breed, although given to occasional flurries of unseemly deference to guests who held high office. Carson was an ingratiatingly lively Puck for a fellow with whitening locks, and he knew better than most how to keep a show moving.

But empty vessels make more sound than full ones, and the same goes for some of the spectrum's hosts and guests. The only certain prophylaxis against prattle and chaff lies in the host's own resources; in his knowledge, understanding, taste, care in picking guests and adroitness in bringing them out;

that, plus his overall sense of proportion, particularly the ability to know when enough is enough of a guest or subject.

There were stalwarts who stood fast against the prevailing winds of fatuity: Carson, Cronkite, Cavett, Douglas, Marlow, Moyers, Champlin, Seidenbaum, Cromie, Terkel, Jackson, Buckley, among others. While Buckley's conservatism now and then touched on the Pleistocene, his programs were well prepared and amounted to a kind of theater. He took on guests who, like himself, were prepared to do battle, and that was eminently fair. No one could deny that Buckley's language was well above the average host's; and if his ideology occasionally drifted to the right of Goldwater, he at least expressed it with flair, loftiness, and outcroppings of erudition. Also gratuitious winking.

I suspect that much of the inconsequential niggling of radio-TV talk shows is inherent in the species of programming. whose unit consists not of a time slot, but a time *slab*. If you impose on even an alert man the task of filling hours on end with improvised talk, the chances are strong that somewhere along the way he will, by sheer attrition of his energy and wit, lose his accustomed poise. Such a thing happened to one of the best men in the medium during observance of our 200th Fourth.

It seems Walter Cronkite was handling the whole day for CBS. (Why he alone should have represented a major network on a major occasion, is another matter.) At intervals throughout the day, Cronkite was host to various guests—a ship's captain, an opera singer and so on. Along toward the middle of this 16-hour Cronkathon, Danny Kaye joined him. Now Kaye is an illustrious citizen of the arts, and Cronkite is certainly one of the first citizens of TV, and you would think that together they would sparkle like a July 4th firework. Alas, they labored and delivered a mouse. Here is what happened:

Kaye, once settled in the guest's seat, announced that he had brought with him several volumes of "research" on the Revolutionary period. He next paid the usual ritualistic compliments on the wonderful job TV was doing and the wonderful job Cronkite was doing, and then there was a commercial break. When the break was over, Cronkite said something to the effect that he understood Kaye had some information on the origin of the name Yankee. "Ah, you've been peeking at my research!" Kaye exclaimed.

"No." Cronkite replied, sounding a little annoyed, "you asked me to ask you." It was an acerbic response to a kidding comment, and it clearly embarrassed Kaye. The exchange was below par for both men, but especially for Cronkite, who after all was Kaye's host. The passage may seem a small detail, but nothing that is transmitted into millions of homes is small. What preceded and followed the exchange was of little import, and the whole episode came across as filler. My point is that only on a spontaneous talk show could two performers as respectable and admired as Kaye and Cronkite have engendered between them a weak half hour.

Of course none of the foregoing constitutes a serious crime. There is no law that says TV or radio spokesmen must be sharp at all times, courteous, informed, intelligent and discreet. But it is saddening that so few offer so little to so many.

I think part of the problem is that both programmers and audiences are over-infatuated with celebrity worship. It is ultimately demeaning to both celebrity and worshipper. The extreme form may be seen in the pathetic spectacle of adorers who wait for hours outside stage doors, or at airports, for a peek at their idol, and those poor souls who scream and faint at the sight of a singer, or who stand under a broiling sun or a storm of confetti to catch a glimpse of a visiting potentate, or general, or some pilot who was first to cross the country flying upside down.

Celebrities are known chiefly for being well known, and they are with us late and soon, but that does not mean they need to leave their specialties to peddle products and fill national time with aimless chatter. If it's sprightly or illuminating conversation one is after, there are thousands of candidates of no celebrity whatever who could do as well or better. Carl Jung, in *Memories, Dreams, Reflections,* wrote, "Encounters with people of many different kinds have been for me incomparably more important than fragmentary conversations with celebrities. The finest and most significant conversations of my life were anonymous."

I am not anti-celebrity (some of my best friends, etc.); I am simply against the exploitation of name and fame in areas where they are not at home, but intruders. I do not for a moment suggest that being a celebrity disqualifies one from intelligent and stimulating conversation. But there are such things as overexposure, being on too long, talking too much and saying too little.

In the beginning was the word. In the end let's not have baloney.

SMITH AND
THE SNOBS

I HEARD A COMPLAINT THE OTHER DAY ABOUT
Jack Smith, whose columns for the *Los Angeles Times* long
ago established him as one of the most ingratiating and witty
essayists ever to indulge. The complainant said he admired
everything about Smith except his name.

I accused my friend of being a name snob, one of the worst
kind. And then I asked if it was the Jack or the Smith he objected to.

"Neither. It's the combination."

"Would you prefer Abou Ben Smith?" I pursued. "Or
Cholmondeley Smith? Or Tennessee Ernie Smith? Cecil
Smith has been taken by a distinguished critic, but how about
Wolfgang Amadeus Smith?"

"You joke," he admonished me, "but at the same time you
help me make my point. Every one of those names has more
color and sticking power than Jack Smith."

"Richard Milhous Smith?"

"An unimpeachable name. But the fact is there are 25,159 Jack and John Smiths in the Los Angeles telephone directories alone. I spent a week counting them. And then think of all the *un*listed Jack Smiths!"

I opened my mouth to reply, but he kept on. "There was once a girl named Gladys Smith, who had the good sense to change her name to Mary Pickford, and she became America's Sweetheart."

I said she would still have been America's Sweetheart if she had remained Gladys Smith, and I reminded him that a major religion, the Mormon, was founded by Joseph Smith.

"Aha!" he cried, "I have you there! How would you like a Redeemer named Jesus Smith? Can you imagine a great faith called Smithianity?"

I said I could, and argued that it would be as valid a name as Mohammedanism or Buddhism or Confucianism, to cite only three religions called after their prophets. At that point we declared a draw, and went on to other matters, like the Watergate hearings and the prospects of the Boston Red Sox if Carl Yastrzemski (probably Polish for Elgin Smith) should start hitting again.

Later I got to thinking about how universal and pervasive are the forms of snobbery. The arts abound in them. So do such widely varied disciplines as advertising, scholarship, criticism, psychoanalysis and gourmandizing. A good example to start with is a perfume by Givenchy. Under a glamorous full-page portrait of Audrey Hepburn runs the legend, "Once she was the only woman in the world to wear this perfume. *L'Interdit*. Created by Givenchy for Audrey Hepburn." The implication is that for some unspecified reason, the period of exclusivity has passed: the aroma ambrosial that once

wafted only from the person of Miss Hepburn may now be
yours for the price of a vial. The operative words in this
thunderclap of snobbery are "the only woman in the world."
Thus it becomes one's *privilege* to buy this scent.

I suspect that women are much more often subjected to this
kind of elitist pitch than men. It is unthinkable, for instance,
that beneath a full-page picture of Hank Aaron or Laurence
Olivier or John Dean III, Fabergé would proclaim that the
gentleman pictured was at one time the only male in the world
allowed to refresh his skin with Brut Lotion.

There there is the department of restaurateurs. Why, in
Omaha, should one be served a menu listing "Chota Jingre
KaSalan," when the item is shrimp curry? Why, in San
Francisco, not notable for its French quarter, should there be
the untranslated entry, "La Poularde Etuvée Aux Morilles
(for 2)", when what they were offering was chicken with
mushrooms? In West Los Angeles I found listed "Guiso de
Carne a la Cordobesa," which turned out to be beef stew. I
also came across a dish called "Ghai Gosht Vindaloo"—not in
Burma, but in Ogunquit, Maine.

In every case where the name of the exotic dish is not translated on the menu, the customer is obliged to ask what it
means. This gives the restaurant staff a one-upsman advantage
which is really not necessary these days, since the management always remains one up in its prices.

There is quite a bit of Ghai Gosht Vindaloo in scholarship,
too, and it is a worse bore even than undeciphered items on
menus. I recently read a book entitled *Cervantes' Women of
Literary Tradition*. Solidly imbedded in a matrix of English
commentary were scores of sources for the women who appear
in *Don Quixote* and other works by Cervantes—all quoted in
the original Spanish, with never a word of translation. This

in effect said to the reader, "If you care enough about Cervantes to read this highly specialized material, you should jolly well know Spanish, and if you don't, I, the author, am not going to waste space and effort translating hundreds of quoted lines, for an ignorant boor too lazy to learn the Spanish tongue."

This is an example of plodding snobbishness. Here now is a specimen of the chic type: Truman Capote, writing on Cecil Beaton in *Vogue,* alluded to a second photographer in the phrase, "Cartier-Bresson is another *tasse de thé* entirely." To have written "cup of tea" would have been to commit a cliché. By shunting the phrase into French, Capote undertook to avoid the cliché. He did not avoid it, he only made it pretentious.

There is to me something ungracious, not only in style but in manners, about the use of words that the writer knows very well are Greek to the general reader. Not long ago a professor of English at UCLA, reviewing a book by Nabokov, used the word tralatitious. He was so proud of that word that a few sentences further on he used the noun form, tralatition. I consulted three dictionaries, one of them unabridged, without being able to find it. A fourth yielded the word, but not, it seemed to me, with much enthusiasm. The ungraciousness with which I charge the professor lies either in his airy assumption that readers are familiar with that fancy term— an unwarranted assumption by any standard—or that if we don't know the meaning of tralatitious we can damn well look it up. (It means metaphoric.) If tralatitious happened to be the exactly right, indispensable word in the context of the professor's review, I would have looked it up with good cheer and a sense of learning something; but since English is the richest of all languages in depth of synonyms, and there are a dozen equally good or better ways of saying the same thing, I felt I had been snobbed upon.

Still another active in-group elitism shelters under the high dome of psychoanalysis. In the texts and vestibules of that discipline one may actually find such terms as "gradiated reciprocation intension reduction" and "content-addressable storage system." The first sounds like space technology; the second, business management. In the comic strip *Peanuts*, the rarely daunted Lucy once explained to a peer, "No book on psychology can be any good if you understand it."

I could go on documenting such varicose forms of snobbery as destroying the plates of beautifully produced books, in order that the editions be rare and high priced. In my view that is merely a reduction of the principle expressed when one of the mad czars of Russia, elated over a masterpiece created by an architectural genius, ordered the architect killed so that there could never again be an edifice like the one he had just built.

Uniqueness has rights and dignities and proper rewards, but when it becomes the slave of caste and privilege and exclusivity, to the accompaniment of tunes on the cash register, then it is demeaned, not ennobled.

There was once a woman in the news named Mrs. O. Just the letter O. I have forgotten whether it was Evelyn O or Harriet O or Desdemona O. (Happy thought: if her name was Olive Odetta O, her initials would be O.O.O.; but never mind.) I wanted to write an ode to her name, and maybe I still will. But in the meantime, Jack Smith, please do not change your name, even if you should be sorely tempted by such rich and delightful ones as Wayne Warga, Bella Stumbo, Fiorello H. LaGuardia, and Ditters von Dittersdorf.

¿BÉISBOL, ANYONE?

MY FRIEND THE SNOB, THE SAME WHO HELD
that a distinguished writer should cast off his name of Jack
Smith because it is too common, is back at it again. He was
until recently a baseball fan—no doubt a carry-over from some
childhood episode, because ordinarily he would not deign to
notice anything so plebeian as a national pastime. Lately he had
been watching the *Game of the Week* on television, and he
became querulous about what he felt was the sport's want of
verve, style and class. "In a word," he complained, "it lacks
panache."

I asked him to give me an example of a sport that has panache.

"Polo."

I objected that polo is a rich man's divertissement, invented
by idle maharajas in the Punjab, and played by mounted snobs
for an audience of seated snobs. I then challenged him to

225

name a popular sport that had panache. He thought for a moment, and his eyes brightened.

"Bullfighting!"

I asked him to amplify. He did. He expanded on the pageant, the drama, the mystique of the bullring. He lingered on the equipage of the *torero,* the embroidery, the waistcoat and sash, the cap with artificial pigtail, the stockinette breeches, the heelless slippers. He spiced his description with colorful condiments of Spanish, savoring each syllable. There is the *alguacil,* he explained, sometimes spelled *alquazil,* who receives the keys to the bullpen (*toril*) and presents dismembered parts of the fallen bull, such as an ear or a tail, to the victorious *matador.* And there are *los chulos, los banderilleros, El Cachetero.* . . .

"Wasn't El Cachetero that bullfighter from Newark who got gored in Tijuana?" I asked.

"No no no, a *cachetero* is the *torero* who finishes off the bull with a short dagger." He went on about the dignity of the worthies who sit in the reserved box of the *ayuntamiento,* about the flagging and wafting and waggling of the *capa,* about the mincing and measured and graceful footwork, about the pass known as the *Verónica.* "*Con capa extendida entre las dos manos,*" he added, remembering to forget that he was speaking to a person who *hablas* sorrowfully little *español.*

"I see your point," I said, letting him think he had successfully planted a *banderilla* in my withers. "But to get back to baseball, has it always been verveless and panacheless, or have you noticed it only lately?"

His answer surprised me. Television, he claimed, has finally exposed the congenital dullness of the game. For the spectator in the ball park, the slack is taken up somewhat by the ambience of the customers, the animal presence of a cheering (or sleeping) crowd, the comforting knowledge that hot dogs and peanuts, the ambrosia of the peasant class, are never far away, and that during the stately pauses of the game, there is opportunity to look around, talk to your neighbors, or futz with (*vagar sin objeto*) a scorecard.

But on television, he went on, there is a merciless drag while the camera rests on the pitcher and he goes through his boring catechism of mannerisms—touching the peak of his cap, putting fingers to mouth, hitching his shoulder, turning his back to the batter, kicking dirt, digging same with toe, pulling his shirt away from his undershirt, removing his cap, placing it back on, touching the peak again to make sure it is there, running his finger around his neck to squeegee beads of perspiration, tugging at the cuff of his pitching arm, crouching to read the catcher's sign, shaking them off with a flick of his glove, nodding approval at last, straightening up, rocking once or twice, and finally delivering the ball. Which is fouled off, whereupon the whole process starts over again.

He paused at this point to light his pipe, and I took advantage of the break to suggest a means of elevating baseball to the level of a panache sport. He was interested. "Simply give names to each of the motions," I proposed, "as the camera picks it up at close range."

"Give me examples."

I lined them up:

—Pitcher fidgets with cap. This could be called the *gorra,* or, if he raises the cap, the *gorrada,* either of which sounds more elegant than its English equivalent.

—Pitcher leans forward and peers in for a sign from the catcher. This is the *escrutinio.*

—Pitcher flicks glove, indicating that he does not agree with the signal. This could be called the *stretta di mano,* or the *Arabella.*

—Pitcher bends down to tie his shoe. This could be called "tying the shoelace."

—Pitcher turns to study a runner on first base. *Pensar primero.*

—Pitcher reviews the situation at second base, which is also occupied by a runner. *Pensar segundo.*

—Pitcher turns and looks at the runner on third base. *Pensar tercero.*

—Pitcher winds up. This is the *molina de viento* (windmill), or the *Isabella.*

—Pitcher throws a curve ball. *Gancho de la trayectoria* (hook of the trajectory) or *Dueña Volante* (The Flying Lady).

—Pitcher watches ball as it sails out of the park (home run). To the pitcher that is the *pelota dolorosa,* to the batter it is simply known as the *jonrón.*

I then went on to suggest that the losing pitcher be humiliated by having the peak of his cap cut off and surrendered to the *compromisario* (umpire), who presents it to the winning pitcher; the latter in turn presents the trophy of triumph to a starlet engaged expressly for the game, who sits behind first base in a place of honor called *palco de gatito* (box of the pussy cat).

My friend was very impatient with my suggestions, and refused to consider that they would incidentally broaden the baseball market to include Hispaniola, the Balearic Islands, and in fact the entire Spanish-speaking world. But we did agree on four points before we broke up our conference and headed for our separate freeways:

1. Boring as the ritualistic fidgets of the pitcher may be, they are not as deadly as the commercials between innings, which sometimes are repeated three or four times in the course of the game.

2. The staff organist at the electric console of the average ball park ranks somewhere between a public nuisance and a public enemy. If these Power Biggses of the diamond must play in frequent spurts, let them at least acquire some new tunes. The California Angels, in their Anaheim chapel, used to (and may still) have an organist who never seemed to rest; there was a steady flak of insipid chatter from his instrument throughout the game, and no one could escape it short of ear-plugs.

3. It is high time (*ya es hora*) that the intentional base on balls (*pasa a primera base*) was foreshortened. A single wide pitch, where the catcher steps out of his position to receive the ball, should signalize the intention of the pitcher to walk the batter, without going through the archaic, time-consuming ceremony of pitching three more balls the same way. It does not take us long to get the idea; what is boring is to watch the intention spelled out four times in succession.

4. A candidate for enshrinement in the archives of the Baseball Hall of Fame is that glorious moment, preserved we hope on videotape, when Tug McGraw, pitcher for the New York Mets, in a pregame interview, insufflated a wad of bubble gum until it obscured both himself and his interviewer, and filled the frame of the TV tube. It was the world's most widely disseminated demonstration of the physical and esthetic properties of *chicle de globo*.

OF PRUNES
AND PERSUASION

THE CALIFORNIA PRUNE ADVISORY BOARD HAS been trying to get us to reconsider the prune. In one of its commercials, two stewardesses on an airplane are discussing a bizarre request by a passenger in seat 12-B. It seems this nut would like some prunes. The request sends them into paroxysms of laughter. Why? Because the prune is so funny. Who in his right mind, one gathers, would want to be seen ingesting a prune? They are still laughing when the vignette fades out. In another sequence, a man calls on a lady in a neighboring apartment. He is carrying an empty cup. The lady assumes he wants to borrow sugar, but when he announces that he was hoping to borrow a few prunes, she bursts into hysterical laughter, and is barely able to splutter, through giggles that almost gag her, that maybe he should try next door. In the third of these dramas, two dese-and-dem workmen are convulsed with merriment by the idea of a laborer resorting to prunes for nourishment. In each case the commercial ends with the moral that all is not ludicrous that is wrinkled: prunes may look ridiculous but they are loaded with iron and valuable vitamins.

My advice to the Prune Advisory Board is that it is not their prunes but their commercials that are ridiculous. The prune is no more comical than the raisin or currant of the dried fig or apricot. Were I not a prune-fancier from a long way back, I might have been persuaded to do the very opposite of what they intended by the commercials—to avoid by all means being seen in public with a prune, lest I be dismissed as a square, a yokel, or a fetishist in need of therapy against a compulsion to feed on mirth-generating prunes.

The Prune Advisory Board, together with the Milk Advisory Board, whose commercials starring Mark Spitz, Phyllis Diller, Diahann Carroll and other beauties have caused me to reduce somewhat my milk consumption, started me thinking of the total phenomenon of persuasion. It is, without any question, one of the most elemental and persistent of all acts of man; moreover it also represents certain acts of God. It is perhaps the oldest art, considering that long before music, painting and needlepoint, it was practiced by virtuosi. The Serpent, without even the benefit of help from an Apple Advisory Board, persuaded Eve to eat of the forbidden fruit. Abraham persuaded no less than his Creator to go easy on Sodom, and in the process (Genesis 18: 22–33) instructed Him in humaneness. Moses, with the help of seven plagues, persuaded Pharoah to let his people go. The object of miracles immemorial has been to persuade skeptics and neutrals of a true belief. The walking on water was not to show off, but to emphasize the power of faith. Peter, after successfully walking some distance in this manner, became frightened by choppy water and cried out for help (Matthew 28: 29–31) whereupon he was chided for lacking faith.

From infancy persuasion operates through reward and punishment (eat it all up, and you'll be strong; be a good girl and Santa will bring you a puppy; do your homework and make the honor roll; practice makes perfect); thus the process is very much a part of us. As we grow older, persuasion becomes diversified: it broadens or sublimates into such modes as inducement, motivation, enticement, urgency, influence, conviction. Whole ideologies and sects rest on the interplay and efficacy of these forces, hence the common descriptive term, "He is of the Baptist [or this, that or the other] *persuasion*."

It is to be expected, then, that the media, which are as much involved in modern life as oil and taxes, should be full up in the techniques and application of persuasion. Madison Avenue rests on the institution as surely as a dome rests on supports. Political and commercial campaigns, the administration of government, missionary activity, the conduct of war, the propagation of credos, the viability of isms, depend upon varying degrees of proselytism.

No place is sacred to the exercise of propaganda—the home, the forum, the school, the press, the radio, the tube, the movie screen, the street corner, the pulpit, even the awards ceremony. When Marlon Brando was voted best actor for his performance as the Mafia chieftain in *The Godfather*, he delegated an Indian maiden to decline the Oscar in his name, in an attempt to persuade viewers of the merits of the cause of Indians then demonstrating at Wounded Knee. Mafia thuggery and Indian rights have little in common, but the platform was vast, and the world was tuned in.

Whether or not the medium is the message, it is certainly the conveyor of the message. But the medium owns its platform. Newspapers run editorials and cartoons, and broadcasters present their management-spokesmen or commentators to speak the corporation's mind. Opponents of their views must scrabble for space in letter columns, or qualify themselves as representatives of some accredited faction in order to get equal time to reply. Failing these resorts, the adversary position must be bought and paid for. Hence the proliferation of political ads, especially in newspapers. A committee of citizens bought a full page in the *Los Angeles Times* to urge the impeachment of Nixon; a southern manufacturer bought a full page in the *Wall Street Journal* to attack Nixon's critics; the president himself, who had prime access to prime time, nevertheless invoked "Operation Candor" in an effort to persuade the country, through the media, that he was, in his own words, not a crook.

Of course, the richer and more powerful the entity, the greater the command of the apparatus of persuasion. Some volleys are almost reply-proof. If a multimillion dollar motion picture promotes some point of view on a social or political issue, or gives expression to its own slant on an aspect of history, it is very expensive business to reply in kind. A documentary filmmaker once felt obliged to produce a desperately earnest rebuttal to what he alleged were gross distortions of truth in the movie *Bonnie and Clyde*. Millions saw the latter film; nobody saw the documentary. There is no such thing as equal time on a movie screen.

The role of media as agent-in-chief of persuasion carries with it certain obvious dangers. For the first time in history most of the masses have largely abandoned the empirical approach to knowledge and understanding. In the old days we tended to find things out for ourselves, we experimented, we read, discussed, weighed, measured, *thought* for ourselves.

MEDIA, EQUIVOKES, SNOBS, PIFFLE

Today we take somebody's word for almost everything: we are manipulated by the most persuasive advertiser, the biggest display, the smoothest or most fatherly men, the administration handout, the sharpest slogan, to buy this shampoo or that candidate, this car or that explanation, to swallow this price hike or that priority.

Not until the flowering of radio and TV could one get three such far-apart minds as William Blake, Walter Lippmann and Norman Mailer to agree on anything. But they do, on the subject of persuasion. First, Blake: "Does a firm persuasion that a thing is so, make it so?"

Lippmann: "When distant and unfamiliar and complex things are communicated to great masses of people, the truth suffers a considerable and often a radical distortion. The complex is made over into the simple, the hypothetical into the dogmatic, and the relative into the absolute."

Mailer: "Each day a few more lies eat into the seed with which we are born, little institutional lies from the print of newspapers, the shockwaves of television, and the sentimental cheats of the movie screen."

I do not hold with Mailer that every day in every way the media set about to lie and cheat; I merely point out the singularity of these views converging over a spread of 150 years.

One could go on, but I forbear. The subject of persuasion in the media is so huge and has so many ramifications that it cannot be exhausted in one seance of this sort. Maybe the year 2000 will be soon enough for a sequel. In the meantime, how about free time for an accredited prune to reply to the slander that, *in situ*, it is a hopelessly laughable misfit among the world's edibles.

TOUGH GUYS

TELLY SAVALAS, WHOSE BALD DOME HAS AL-most become a national monument like the granite heads of Mount Rushmore, looks out from a full-page ad in a national magazine and, as he pushes the knot of his necktie into place, says, "So don't try a Twinjector shave. It's no skin off my face."

The expression on Telly's face in this ad is one of restrained annoyance, as though convinced that if, after he has been urging you to try a Twinjector, you still decline, it is because you must be stupid, obstinate, poor in spirit and antiprogress. The tone is basically rude, like that of the liquor ad which went something like, "If you can buy a better bourbon at this price, go ahead and buy it." Such thrusts, which amount to saying, "You know what you can do with your preferences," aggressively assume superiority, a claim supported by no other standard than the shove of the advertisement.

Whiskey and razors are not the only products that occasionally elect to be served by rudeness. Some time back a cigarette, whose name I successfully block from memory, had as its TV spokesman an actor who looked and behaved like a —well, the only euphemism that comes to mind is snot. In private life the actor may be courteous and perhaps even charming, but on the tube he was required to be overbearing. Although the script of these cigarette commercials varied from week to week (a different locale and female were involved in each) the situation and action were always the same. The scenario was simple: Scowling he-man takes a pack of cigarettes and prepares to light up. Attractive woman sees this, and asks if she may have one. Hero arrogantly turns his back on her and walks away. I felt no upwelling of sympathy for the spurned petitioner—for her or any other woman who would approach a stranger to bum a cigarette from him; but the rejection was so insolent as acted out on the tube, so gratuitously gross, that I almost forgave the dame's imprudence for the punk's impudence.

That little model of social behavior, transmitted by a giant network into millions of homes, was there for all Americans to witness. Television does not have to broadcast palpable violence in order to work a desultory effect on impressionable young people. Rudeness does very well as a stand-in.

Of course cigarette advertising has since been banned from TV, but some tobacco companies cling stubbornly to the image of rugged manliness in the printed media. A recent ad campaign shows a craggy, broad-shouldered, square-jawed young man dressed in an open-necked safari suit, staring at you very sullenly. He is in the act of drawing a cigarette from a pack whose label, naturally, is held toward camera. The look is so grim and tough that you figure it would go better with the act of drawing a gun, and you suspect that upon completing the transfer of cigarette from pack to mouth, the model will demand to know who the hell you are and what the hell you are doing there.

Marlboro is another cigarette that insists on brawn. Perhaps because the name is aristocratic, suggesting a long line of effete earls and dukes, the house of Marlboro found it strategic to depict its clientele as the quintessence of machismo. Marlboro smokers live and work in a region named Marlboro Country—western canyons and ranges where seldom is heard a discouraging word (let alone a discouraging cough) and the skies are not cloudy all day. Since landscapes do not of themselves smoke, except when set afire by careless smokers, the term Marlboro Country refers to the vaqueros who roam it. You are invited to assume that they are all smoking the right brand.

But there are women models in some ads too—full-page color portraits of she-smokers. The few I have seen might as well be men. One of them, dressed in Levis and a blue denim shirt, wears the same threatening aspect as the hombre cited above. She has no truck with lipstick, has been nowhere near a flask of shampoo, and her eyes are not made up, which would all be fine if she weren't glaring at us so balefully. The lady is not hard, but we gather she is tough.

Just as violence is nightly merchandised on TV, so is toughness distributed all over the entertainment spectrum. Tough sleuths, cops, bad guys, good guys, beauties who can throw a karate chop that would fell an ox; strong silent heroes like Charles Bronson, Clint Eastwood, Burt Reynolds, John Wayne and Robert Mitchum, who have a total of two expressions among them, and who are capable of infinite toughness in infinite script situations.

Perhaps the drive to win at any cost, which permeates business and sports from Little League baseball on up to the Super Bowl, is at the core of the macho syndrome. Football coaching tends to attract a particularly aggressive breed, and sometimes there seems to me little to choose from, in approach, between types like the military drillmasters who beat or exhaust recruits in the name of discipline and toughness, and a coach like the one described by Ted Green in the *Los Angeles Times*. This was Mr. Kush of Arizona State, "billed as 'the meanest coach in college football.'"

Green quoted a player as saying that long overtime practice drills (typical: a two-and-a-half-hour scrimmage in 90-degree heat) "were more brutal and head-rattling than any of our games." Once, Green wrote, a running back skidded out of bounds into barbed wire which separated the practice field from a creek, and when some teammates started to run to his aid, Kush shouted, "No one go over there. We can't worry about him." Another player recalled a game when "someone dropped a catchable pass and Kush 'called everyone [to stand] around him and the guy, so no one could see, and beat the crap out of him.'" General Patton was disciplined for less, but in the tiger cages of "entertainment" apparently anything goes; and football is entertainment for the masses.

One does not have to be tough to be strong or virile. Even a professional bruiser like Muhammad Ali, world heavyweight boxing champion, kidded his strength and the power of his anesthetizing right jab, both in and out of the ring. He was the least silent strong man in the history of the sport.

I have a notion that Goliath may have been a nice mild Philistine farm boy who had the bad luck to run into David's marksmanship. Big men are usually gentle—they don't have to flout their strength; it is visible.

Tough Guys

There seems to me something suspiciously defensive about the need to proclaim and demonstrate toughness and virility, some nagging sense of insecurity perhaps, as in the example of the up-and-at-'em macho husband in *Tea and Sympathy*.

I think the most boring thing about the sock-biff-bang serials on TV, the revengers on the big screen, the mayhem binges as in pictures like *The Dirty Dozen,* is not the sheer mechanical repetitiousness of jaw-busting, chair-breaking, window-shattering, car-smashing, skull-fracturing, knifing, shooting and strangling, but the *mindlessness* of it all. There is plenty of blood and carnage in *War and Peace* and in *Hamlet* and *Macbeth,* but a lot more mind is exercised than muscle.

I have nothing against strong men as such. Not even strong silent men. I'm just against strong silent dummies who are "tough" (i.e., violent) for the sake of cheap sensation.

The conjugations of men's strength are as many and various as those of women's beauty. Helen Keller was as plain as apple pie, but to me she was more beautiful than Helen of Troy or Grace of Monaco. Mohandas Gandhi may not have been able to lift a full grocery bag, but he was a strong man. So were all those people across the centuries who sacrificed comfort, convenience, fortunes and sometimes their lives in the cause of human dignity and decency. Not one of them ever did it with toughness, or an eye on the box office.

ETERNAL TRIANGLE: SEX, ART, AND THE ESTABLISHMENT

FEW OF US HAVE TROUBLE DEFINING AN ART-
ist, and sex is conjugated by just about everybody, but one
must establish what is meant by the Establishment. It is an
oversimplification to call it the Institution of the Ins, the top
dogs and the fat cats, although they all belong. The dictionaries, including the $25 ones, agree on certain qualities of
establishment, such as those of being settled, recognized,
accepted, and permanent. Even in card games, "to establish"
means to gain such control of a suit that one can win every
remaining trick . . . a fond and persistent dream of every
establishment.

The establishment is all-embracing. It's the Empire, the
Presidency, the Holy See, the Shah, the Kremlin, ITT; City

(Lecture delivered by Corwin at the University of North Carolina,
Chapel Hill)

Eternal Triangle: Sex, Art, and the Establishment

Hall, the Army, the Navy, the Police, the Courts, the Censors, the Critics, the System, the Sacraria of the Networks, the Baronetcies of Steel and Oil.

But in its very nature, the establishment presents a paradox. Although it is rooted in, and dedicated to, the object of its own permanence, yet for all its power and entrenchment, it is less permanent than many supposedly frailer organisms and works all about us, especially works of art. Thrones are overturned, administrations swept out of office, systems destroyed, critics forgotten. Navies are sunk and armies are slaughtered —by other armies and navies to be sure. For if there is one thing a successful establishment cannot tolerate, it is another successful establishment that competes with it. That is what the average war is about.

Of course the oldest and most reputable Establishment of all is God: By common consent He's the uttermost symbol of control and permanence. Yet even God has been rumored to be dead, or missing in action. But assuming He is alive and taking prayers, He has been reformed from time to time, as we know from the history of theology. It might be said, after first apologizing to Lincoln, that the common people must love God, they made so many of Him.

Now theoretically, at the very antipodes to the establishment, stands the artist. I say theoretically, because there has been a great deal of interaction and crossing of enemy lines. But if the artist has any originality in him at all, by nature he resists all that is settled and permanent and regimented; he learns the established rules of his art in order to be able to break them creatively.

The artist's whole raison d'etre, his justification to himself for being alive, his justification to society for sitting in a chair and writing, or playing a musical instrument instead of ploughing a field or digging coal, is the belief that if and when he expresses his unique self uniquely he will be creating something beautiful, or true, or needed, or wanted, or perhaps useful to others, if only to give them pleasure.

The artist is nothing if not individual. And yet the establishment, whose instinct is to nullify the indivdual, to homogenize and lump and level us all, to make numbers of us and feed us into computers, this same establishment is very much attracted to the artist—when he/she can be useful to it. The establishment of the Church was responsible for whole prodigies of art, because the art glorified the Church. In ancient Egypt, sculptors and painters lived high because their art deified the Pharaohs. In Greece and Rome art celebrated the gods. In modern Russia artists glorify the party and the proletariat, and rarely stray from dogma, with results of almost uniform dullness and drabness. Happy, down the ages, has been the artist who could exalt the Holy Cow and the Sacred Cat and the Supreme Panjandrum in good conscience.

The establishment is terribly careful of its image, and who more than the artist is expert in image-making? Not since Narcissus has there been such an awareness of one's own image as there now exists on every level—politically, militarily, industrially, in the arts and sciences.

The whole vast apparatus of public relations, the golden commissions of Madison Avenue, the astronomic advertising budgets, all exist for the purpose of creating and maintaining carefully calculated images of one or another Establishment; for images are translatable into prestige, into power, and above all, profit. Images can be changed. Even images of mundane things like groceries. Oleomargarine once had a bad image— the butter interests saw to that. Now, by law, oleomargarine has citizenship. For a long time, the baseball establishment had a strictly Caucasian image, as white as Lester Maddox, but Jackie Robinson—in the role of the artist—changed that for us. The image of Hollywood used to be that of a suburban Gomorrah, saved from the wrath of God only because it borders on Beverly Hills; today Hollywood is almost as respectable as Omaha because the producers' establishment worked very hard to change its image. When it serves the establishment to do so, it embraces the artist; and when it serves the artist, he embraces the establishment.

The artist who for profit identifies himself with something in which he does not believe, who rationalizes his support of the unjust cause, who runs with the hounds and toadies to the establishment, is rewarded in many ways—if not by money, then at the very least by immunities against the frowns, the disfavor or the persecution of the establishment.

The establishment can be very fierce about denying the artist the right to be heard or seen, and even the right to live. In the ancient Judaic code, the graven image was forbidden under penalty of death. In early Christianity, drama was considered idolatrous, as having too much contact with temporal life, and it was banned. Eight centuries lapsed after the death of Christ before anyone dared to write plays—even pro-Christian plays. The Puritan Commonwealth shut down theaters in the 17th Century.

It is a universal trait of rigid establishments to destroy the nonconforming artist. The Nazis burned books. The Russians, Czechs, Red Chinese, demand that their artists toe the party line, always in the "best interests" of the state, always to protect their image of themselves.

In the disgraceful period through which we passed during the zenith of McCarthy and McCarran and the blacklists and witch-hunts, the artist was a prime target. Millions were

spent keeping tabs on the patriotism of writers, actors, directors, singers, dancers. Ministers and officeholders and educators were attacked too, but artists made the juiciest venison to
bring back from the hunt. The entire artist population was
divided into the loyal and disloyal, with self-appointed monitors and inquisitors from among their own ranks. The networks maintained "security" executives to make sure that no
hairdresser or grip or actor whose name appeared on anybody's
private or corporate or semi-public blacklist could subvert the
reign by setting someone's hair, or moving a cable, or enacting
a role.

As a general rule, to have your painting hang in the palace
you must flatter the subject. Lyndon Johnson, when president,
rejected an oil painting of himself because, as he said, it disgusted him. In other words it did not match his image of himself, and thus could not qualiy as an official portrait. It is to
the everlasting honor of the Spanish throne in Goya's time,
that he was permitted to paint his homely King and the rest of
a spectacularly unprepossessing royal family, with all their
wens and warts and orthodontic calamities on full display.

So the establishment and the artist are not committed to
be enemies. They can be symbiotic. Church and state have
proven that many times over, and so have occasional rich
givers and lordly patrons. One always hopes for a benign
establishment, and there have been a number of them.

The fact is, with all its frailties and arrogances and abuses,
we cannot do without an establishment. It is simply not
feasible for us all to live in a happy, whappy environment;
unfortunately life is not one big love-in, notwithstanding
the official recognition given the painter Robert Indiana by
the U.S. Post Office when it printed millions of reproduc-
tions of his famous canvas of the word LOVE in the form of

vivid red, green and blue eight-cent stamps. The public licked the back of this issue lovingly; LOVE carried letters for us; it was a moment of reprieve from postal asceticism before the rates went up again.

The bottom line, as they say on the bourse, is for each of us, in and out of authority, to see that the establishment keeps its nose and record clean. In which process the artist helps as gadfly, conscience, teacher, interpreter, and, as Shelley claimed, unacknowledged legislator of the world.

Now offhand, sex may seem an odd companion of the two other angles in my triangle, but they do have working relationships. The establishment legislates sex; the scientist makes actuarial tables and writes books about it; the artist celebrates it and tries to enjoy it. His celebration takes many forms—in painting, from the lady wrestlers of Rubens to the geometrical nudes of Picasso; in literature, from the chasteness of Elizabeth Barrett Browning counting the ways she loves, to Fanny Hill counting the lays she loves; in theater, from *Romeo and Juliet* to *Let My People Come*; in film, from *Seventh Heaven* to *Deep Throat*.

For in sex relations, as perhaps in no other area of human affairs, hypocrisy and sanctimoniousness have been thoroughly compounded. The established church, which usually meant the state, for centuries made of sex a furtive and unclean subject. Sex was something a high-minded person did without. The nobler or holier one's character, the farther removed he was from any thought of sex. D. H. Lawrence was disgusted by all this:

> *Whoever the God was that made us, he made us complete. He didn't stop at the navel and leave the rest to the devil.*

The editors of a standard edition of the Bible strain in their chapter headings to make us believe that *The Song of Solomon* is not an ardent love poem but rather an allegory of the love of Christ for the Church. The painters, sculptors and poets of Christianity went along with the hierarchy, either sincerely or because they knew what side their commissions were buttered on. They populated whole paradises, and did so with a sublime beauty for which we are grateful.

Niagaras of art flowed out of Christianity, as also out of pagan, oriental, and other theocracies. In all but the erotic religions of India and primitive Africa, where the body and its delights were considered gifts of the gods and not snares of the devil, sex was off limits to the artist. And to trespass against the interdictions of the priesthood could be fatal.

It was the establishment of Leviticus, not any artist, that stoned to death the adulterer and whoever uncovered a forbidden nakedness. It was Calvin, and no artist, who executed a young man in Geneva for possessing a small picture of a nude. The artist alone was able to outflank the establishment; only he could evade the prurience of the censors, and then only through the genius of his art. In the darkest era of sexual abnegation, the artist made of nakedness a glory . . . so much so that not even a powerful church, practiced in asceticism, would presume to fig-leaf the David of Michelangelo.

The artist has always been a leavening agent in the ferments that take place periodically within the establishment. In the respect of sex, he always has an advantage: the establishment has to be on the defensive; there is nothing it can do to turn a planetary tide. Love is the most plentiful and cheering of all the world's natural resources, and the artist happens to be its leading spokesman and commissioner. A good example of the problems of authority in dealing with this intriguing element in our lives, is the case of the motion picture industry.

Hollywood at one time felt obligated to set up its own censorship. It devised a Code of morality. But writers, directors and producers kept chipping away at the Code, evading and defying it. And then, when the major studios lost their monopolistic power, more and more writers, actors and directors created their own studios by simply renting space, and so they moved into the establishment, and became part of it. At which point the Code, for all practical purposes, disintegrated. No longer need the movie heroine be a neuter of washed-out libido. No longer did the virginity rites of the Doris Day pictures mark the frontier outposts of sex on films. Hardcore porno films were perfectly free to travel down sewers in glass-bottomed boats, sometimes under expert navigation.

The sexual revolution resulted from a combination of many forces, including Freud and Kinsey and the bomb, but not least was the influence of the artist—through movies, plays, novels, TV, and song lyrics. There are good and bad things about the revolution, and the bad is obvious—the downgrading of sex to a cheap and sniggering, voyeuristic pastime. But a draconic Puritanism can be a greater incentive to prurience than anything carried in the junk-filled newsstands, or written by Ovid, the Marquis de Sade, or Henry Miller.

Throughout history, most despotic establishments have been prim. Our own Puritan society was inhuman and graceless, and left scars that are even now being treated in the offices of psychiatrists. The Nazis, when they occupied Paris, immediately abolished the brothels. They were very proper about sex, while at the same time they were making lampshades of human skin, and destroying millions of lives in gas chambers. The Red Chinese and Soviet regimes are also prudish about sex. The otherwise ebullient Khrushchev was revolted by an innocent can-can number on a Hollywood sound stage. The Greek government of the late 60's was almost psychopathically demure, and thus diametrically in contrast to the Athens of Aristophanes and the great sculptors of the undraped human form.

All through history, vested moral interests have been grudging and restrictive against the most universal expression of love, through sex, while at the same time they have condoned the most universal expression of hate, through war. Sex as a source of pleasure, as distinct from its services to procreation, has been frowned upon, openly or tacitly, by the establishment. But at the same time, violence as an instrument of national policy, has been blessed. The hypocrisy of regarding sex as sinful if practiced in the name of pleasure, while regarding murder as virtuous if practiced in the name of the state, has been manifest to a growing number of people for some time. It did not sit well with a young generation that saw 60 million human beings slaughtered in two world wars, and were aware that this figure could be tripled in the first hours of a third world war. Small wonder they rebelled, and painted LOVE in psychedelic lettering on blank walls. "Make love, not war," they cried.

But now there exist prospectuses for establishments of the future. Holy men, visionaries, poets, have projected many administrations of heaven and hell. More recently, Aldous Huxley and George Orwell gave us awesome glimpses of possibilities here on earth. These visions have in common a loosely speculative stance. They are inexact guesses as to how things will be run in another life, or in our own future—guesses that have nothing in them of slide-rule, test-tube, computer, or electronic microscope. It is only lately that geneticists, cyberneticists, cryogenicists, and biologists— especially biologists—have become very specific about available techniques for shaping our new world. If we are to take these technologists seriously—something we are obliged to do on the basis of past and present performance—then we must come to very solemn considerations about a scientific cabinet sitting at the controls of mankind.

The overall prospect of the scientists is called (by them) The Human Agenda; the sexual part of it is called The New Biology. Every time I read, or hear, an augury of the new biology—and this seems to happen about once a month— I am reminded of Herman Melville's comment about Ralph Waldo Emerson. "Notwithstanding his merit," said Melville, "I could readily see in Emerson a gaping flaw. It was the insinuation that, had he been alive in those days when the world was made, he might have offered some valuable suggestions."

The biologists are now offering valuable suggestions. Whether they are welcome suggestions is the proper concern of us all. At first blush, not many of us would cavil at the allure of what they have projected in recent pronouncements —a world that is universally educated, and relieved of ethnic differences; a world of fixed population and universally high standards of living; a world in which knowledge can be inoculated by needle; a world in which electrophoretic devices weed out unwanted chromosomes and predetermine sex; a world in which identical genotypes can be recreated from the dead, so that we may have any number of living facsimilies of Tutankhamen or Shakespeare or Einstein or Idi Amin or Elizabeth Taylor among us, at will, and at all times, if we so desire. All of these prospects have been announced, along with projections of infinite possibilities for computerizing art and esthetics.

I believe it is not only possible but necessary to cavil at the allure of all this. First, a world of universal education is a shining prospect, except for the always variable standards of what constitutes education, and whether education as we know it has been any forceful deterrent to the crimes of humanity. Few countries in history were as educated as Germany before and even under Hitler. I am afraid that the only universal education this is mandatory today is the one that H. G. Wells had in mind when he said that human history becomes more and more a race between education and catastrophe.

A consistently high standard of living has not made the country of Sweden any happier, as its consistently high incidence of suicide would indicate. And one has no trouble in not confusing Tokyo, a very rich city, with ancient Athens, a relatively poor city, in terms of their services to mankind.

Granted it is pleasant to contemplate a world relieved of the strain of ethnic differences. But if the entire population of the globe were one vast, miscegenated mass, it would no more guarantee epidemic peace and good will than the racial homogeneity of white Americans obviated the Civil War. Ethnic identity did not prevent any of the wars between Caucasians exclusively, Asiatics exclusively, Amazonian Indians or American Indians or Indian Indians exclusively.

A world of fixed population would of course be a great improvement over what we now have, but this plank of the New Biology does not belong with the others, since the techniques for achieving birth control are not conjectural but are already at hand, and the question is political and educational rather than scientific.

Eternal Triangle: Sex, Art, and the Establishment

Concerning the weeding out of unwanted chromosomes and the predetermination of sex, it was all anticipated by Aldous Huxley in *Brave New World,* along with dangers so obvious and horrendous as to need no elaboration. But the incarnation of genotypes of Tutankhamen and Shakespeare and Peter the Great would seem no better than a cruel jest at the expense of whatever soul—call it person if you will—occupies the frame and visage of whatever celebrity we concoct out of the archives. To create a man in the exact image of Julius Caesar or Milton or Beethoven without (we are warned) the genius of the prototype, would certainly be of interest—but of what interest, to whom? Of technical interest to scientists, of course; of sentimental interest to historians; of morbid interest to wax museums, which would be put out of business by this; and of a vulgar, gaping interest to the rest of the world's fixed population—unless, that is, the envisioned universal education will have weaned us all away from this sort of sideshow curiosity. Imagine the discomfort of a neo-Isaac Newton, knowing of the intellectual fame of his ancestral daddio, yet himself able to comprehend only comic books.

I read a serious prospectus on computerized esthetics, by which a machine might be programmed to paint like Mondrian or Vermeer or van Gogh, or whomever. It suggested that the impulses, style, brushwork, and color of any artist of the past might be programmed into an apparatus which would then turn out canvases for delivery to dealers, collectors, museums and hotel rooms. It held that artistic creativity is a sentimental and arbitrary concept, which implies that it is therefore expendable or replaceable. This may be so, but I wonder how the new world is going to retrain millions of sentimentalists like myself who have been brought up to appreciate hand-made Sistine Chapels. Could a transistorized El Greco be programmed to paint a portrait that a replicated Lyndon Johnson would approve?

The injection of knowledge by needle is another vision of the New Biology, and to me a symptom of a science so transfixed by materialism that it dreams of ultimates in expediency. Times means money, and money is the God of a profit-hugging society, and if one can avoid years of formal education by having knowledge pumped into a host overnight, why think of the boy- and man-hours, the girl- and woman-hours saved for other pursuits not specified in the blueprints. Inoculable knowledge would be the ideal tool of dictatorship—to fill the heads of the masses with a carefully selected and controlled curriculum. Still, it would be wonderful to be able to go to your doctor for a shot of differential calculus. The only trouble with a few cc's of concentrated knowledge in the blood is that, even if it gets past the chemical action of surprised glands, and an off-guard liver, or is not oxidated into ignorance through the lungs, such knowledge would be as inhuman and mechanical in the brain as though it were stored in a machine —unless it were accompanied by understanding. But I have not yet seen understanding proposed on any biological level, glandular, chromosomal or electrophoretic. Instant knowledge, yes; instant creativity, yes; instant understanding, no.

Still another spoor of biological investigation under pursuit is that of the rearrangement of facilities for human gestation, whereby a woman, having enjoyed the games associated with conception, might park her embryo in another woman's womb for development and delivery, while she, party of the first part, goes about what we can only assume to be more important business or pleasure. While this commends itself on the same moral scale as a man hiring another to fight for him, which has been done in the past, it does have at least one refreshing aspect: we can look forward to surrogate mothers —the egg-hatchers—banding together to form the first labor union biologically worthy of the name.

Also we are told of the possibility of each human possessing both male and female organs, with both sets in working order. Beyond doubling the sexual-biological option now at the disposal of each of us, I see no particular value to hermaphroditism, which up to now the sciences of medicine and psychiatry have been treating as an undesirable condition by resolving the ambivalence one way or the other, through chemical or surgical means. Now the reverse of this is put on the human agenda—the making of still another sexual type.

Too many scientists—certainly not all, but too many—tend to live in a vacuum depleted of vital concern with the consequences of their work. They will make bombs or poison gas or silly putty or neohomunculi or cobalt warheads with equal dedication for Reds, blackshirts, monarchists, Hindus, Moslems and Republicans. Their rationale is that science is pure, it is a kind of sacred abstraction above the squall of the forum and the crud of the battlefield. There seems to be little common ground between the scientist and the artist—so far from a community of interest that machines are conceived by the scientist to do away with creativity.

Science is traditionally credited with having exerted the greatest influence on life, and no doubt it has been great. But the influence has too often been degrading or degenerating. A man doesn't have to walk any more, or open doors, or climb stairs, or get up from a chair to change a TV channel, or even brush his teeth with wrist motion. Today a well man can have all the advantages of being an invalid—and by having them, he becomes one.

Beyond the very welcome contributions science has made to

ease man's physical burdens, beyond the glorious achievements
of chemistry and medicine, mechanics and electronics, science
has addressed itself to services whose intrinsic or ultimate
value are debatable—it has increased speed, coddled creature
comforts, improved techniques for imposing conformity, and
made certain that we at last have the capacity literally to destroy the earth.

The scientist is off by himself. Both he and we tend to forget that the artist is and always has been a far greater influence on society; that art is not a refuge from life, or an alterna-
tive to it; that the greatest force in the world remains not
nuclear fission but the conscience and will of man, and that of
all the agents that act upon this force, art has the best credits,
whether it be the art of the anonymous poets who wrote the
Bible, or the ennobling drama of Shakespeare, or the sculptors
of the Congo or the painters of the caves—each communicated something treasurable to all who have eyes and ears,
including children who cannot understand cybernetics; each
continues to exert an influence on our lives.

One may ask whether Charles Dickens did not have more
influence on the England of his time than his great scientist
contemporaries, John Herschel and Joseph Lister; whether
Charlie Chaplin is not a healthier influence than the inventory
of the electronic eavesdropper; whether Eero Saarinen or Carl
Sandburg or Benjamin Britten or Samuel Beckett have not
given more of lasting and felicitous value to the world than
color television. Against this kind of comparison, I hear the cry
value judgment! like an indictment, as though there were
something reprehensible about such judgment. The scientist
would like to have us accept his work as beyond the purview
of value judgment, including human value. But he has no

right to except immunity from the concerns of humanity, from the necessities, the obligations and the fate of humanity, for he is part of humanity.

There are of course some people who believe that nothing should be done for the first time, and I am not among them. But there *are* certain things it might be better not to try for a first time—scientific things, such as a formula that stands biology on its head, or embarrasses nature; or a Doomsday machine of the type envisioned by certain physicists; or bacteriological warfare.

Of what value is an extra-organismic brain unless we make proper use of the still insufficiently understood conventional brain that is standard equipment? Of what use are all these radical and brave projections unless we can find our way through the labyrinths created by existing technology? No game of anatomical chairs, as to what generation of frozen sperm fertilizes what crop of eggs, or whose uterus is host to what fetus, or whose kidney is spliced into what plumbing, none of this will have much value if the world into which the New Biology is ushered is the same old money-grubbing, land-grabbing, power-ploying and conformizing place that it is.

Admittedly we ask an extremely difficult thing of the scientist when we expect him to be arbiter and adjudicator of his own invention. He cannot always foresee the use to be made of his work. The Wright brothers at Kitty Hawk could not have been thinking of bombing cities back to the Stone Age; Mergenthaler, who invented the Linotype machine, can hardly be blamed for the yellow press; Lee DeForest is in no way responsible for the soap opera.

Since there is hardly a formula, process or invention which cannot be debased or perverted, like using a telephone to make obscene calls, or electric current for the electric chair, the question comes down to the end to which we elect to put the products of the laboratory.

It has been said that the nemesis of man is not science but war; that new weapons do not of themselves create new wars, they only make them more terrible. But that, I think, is splitting hairs, and is not necessarily true. The military mind likes nothing better than a chance to experiment, to rehearse, test and prove new weapons under optimum conditions. This is in fact an echo of the scientific process. The guinea pig in these experiments is always world peace, and the dispensable white rats and monkeys are you and me.

It is not necessary or desirable to throttle science, to blunt its ardor or curb its imagination. What needs throttling, blunting and curbing above all is war, and to that end everybody must contribute and participate—but especially the scientist. He has the training and the instinct to seek and find solutions, he has the grades and the degrees. But where are the humanist scientists in the councils of government? Why are they not in the open meetings of the United Nations as well as in the closed chambers of Oak Ridge? Should the billions of dollars and rubles for crash programs go first to outer space, or can we spare a franc or two for the few struggling communities of scientific and humanistic conscience—the Institutes of Princeton and Stanford, and the cultural conclaves of the major universities in the world?

In the interim, the scientist, in his sterilized, dustless, dehumanized laboratory, can be expected to go on piling wonder on wonder until, as has been suggested, we get fresh Picassos from IBM and Phillips. If all these glistening new achievements were to be plugged into an orderly world, in which a man had concern for his fellow man, in which you could drive a safe car on a safe highway, in which a quarter of a billion dollars a year were not still being spent to promote and sell a carcinogenic weed, in which the world did not awaken every other morning to read of new acts of terrorism; if all of the proposed biologic virtuosity were to be introduced to a world that had ceased to pollute itself and diminish man, then we could accept with less anxiety the perhaps inevitable arrival of the New Biology. But until we show signs of maturing enough to handle adequately the Old Biology, and of being able to control the fearsome instruments and engines that have already been delivered to us by the establishment, I am afraid that in the scale of human values, a busload of humane artists outweighs the combined government bureaus of all the national capitals in the world.

AROUND THE HORN

WATCHING TV COMMERCIALS IS NOT MY ELEC-
tive indoor sport, and I generally do not quote them in support of the humanities, but there is one spot that I deck with
honor. In it, a mild, middle-aged motorist pulls up to an inter-
section and stops for a red light. While he is waiting for the
light to change, another car stops alongside. At the wheel is
a fetching blonde. She looks at our man invitingly, and ges-
tures for him to incline his ear as though to whisper some
titillating message. The man straightens his tie, rearranges his
face to look as debonair as possible, and sticks his head out of
the window to hear what she has to suggest.

Her smile vanishes. Instead of the anticipated purr, she
snarls at him, "Why don't you fix your muffler?" The man
pulls back like a turtle into its carapace, abashed. Of course
the commercial is to sell mufflers, but that girl speaks for
legions of her countrywomen and countrymen, including me.

258